# REFORMATION, EXPLORATION, AND EMPIRE

Volume 4

FRANCE–INVENTIONS AND INVENTORS

an imprint of

www.scholastic.com/librarypublishing

Published by Grolier,
an imprint of Scholastic Library Publishing,
Sherman Turnpike
Danbury, Connecticut 06816

Set ISBN 0-7172-6071-2
Volume 4 ISBN 0-7172-6075-5

Library of Congress Cataloging-in-Publication Data

Reformation, exploration, and empire.
    p. cm.
    Contents: Vol. 1. Academies–Catherine de Médicis —
v. 2. Catholic church–daily life — v. 3. Decorative arts–
fortifications — v. 4. France–inventions and inventors —
v. 5. Ireland–manufacturing — v. 6. Maps and
mapmaking–Orthodox church — v. 7. Ottoman Empire–
printing — v. 8. Privacy and luxury–sculpture — v. 9.
Servants–textiles — v. 10. Thirteen Colonies–Zwingli.
    Includes bibliographical references and index.
    ISBN 0-7172-6071-2 (set : alk. paper) — ISBN 0-7172-
6072-0 (v. 1 : alk. paper) — ISBN 0-7172-6073-9 (v. 2 :
alk. paper) — ISBN 0-7172-6074-7 (v. 3 : alk. paper) —
ISBN 0-7172-6075-5 (v. 4 : alk. paper) — ISBN 0-7172-
6076-3 (v. 5 : alk. paper) — ISBN 0-7172-6077-1 (v. 6 :
alk. paper) — ISBN 0-7172-6078-X (v. 7 : alk.paper) —
ISBN 0-7172-6079-8 (v. 8 : alk.paper) — ISBN 0-7172-
6080-1 (v. 9 : alk. paper) — ISBN 0-7172-6081-X (v. 10 :
alk. paper)
    1. History, Modern—16th century—Encyclopedias,
Juvenile. 2. History, Modern—17th century—
Encyclopedias, Juvenile. 3 Renaissance—Encyclopedias,
Juvenile. 4 Civilization, Modern—17th century—
Encyclopedias, Juvenile. 5 Reformation—Encyclopedias,
Juvenile. I. Grolier (Firm)

D228.R46 2005
909'.5'03—dc22                                    2004063255

For information address the publisher:
Grolier, Sherman Turnpike,
Danbury, Connecticut 06816

### FOR THE BROWN REFERENCE GROUP

| | |
|---|---|
| Project Editor: | Emily Hill |
| Deputy Editor: | Tom Webber |
| Picture Researcher: | Susy Forbes |
| Maps: | Darren Awuah |
| Design Manager: | Lynne Ross |
| Design: | Q2A Solutions |
| Production Director: | Alastair Gourlay |
| Editorial Director: | Lindsey Lowe |
| Senior Managing Editor: | Tim Cooke |
| Consultant: | Prof. James M. Murray |
| | University of Cincinnati |

Printed and bound in Singapore

# ABOUT THIS SET

This is one of a set of 10 books about the key period of western history from around 1500 to around 1700. The defining event of the age was the Reformation, the attempt to reform the Catholic church that resulted in a permanent split in western Christianity. The period was also marked by the European exploration and colonization of new lands, profound political change, and dynamic cultural achievement.

The roots of the Reformation lay in a tradition of protest against worldliness and corruption in the Catholic church. In 1517 the German Augustinian monk Martin Luther produced a list of criticisms of Catholicism and sparked a protest movement that came to be known as Protestantism. The reformers broke away from Catholicism and established new Protestant churches. In response the Catholic church launched the Counter Reformation, its own program of internal reforms.

Religious change had a profound political influence as Protestantism was adopted by various rulers to whom it offered a useful way to undermine Europe's existing power structures. The period was one of intolerance, persecution, and almost continuous warfare. Meanwhile new approaches to religion combined with the spread of printing and increased literacy to produce a knowledge revolution in which new ideas flourished about science, art, and humanity's place in the universe.

Changes in Europe had a lasting effect on events elsewhere. Spanish conquistadors overthrew vast empires in the Americas, while Catholic missionaries spread Christianity in Africa, the Americas, and Asia. Gradually lands in the east and the west were penetrated and colonized by Europeans. These and other important changes, such as the development of international trade, great cultural achievements, and the spirit of learning, are explored in detail in each volume.

While focusing mainly on Europe, the set also looks at important developments across Africa, Asia, and the Americas. Each entry ends with a list of cross references to related entries so that you can follow up particular topics. Contemporary illustrations give a fuller picture of life during the Reformation. Each volume contains a glossary, a "Further Reading" list that includes websites, a timeline, and an index covering the whole set.

# Contents

## Volume 4

# FRANCE

In the 16th century France was weakened by wars with the Hapsburgs and ravaged by civil wars inspired by religion. In the 17th century, however, the Bourbon kings centralized power, and France gradually became the most powerful country in Europe.

For nearly 1,000 years the kings of France had come from the Capet family, either directly, or through the related families of Valois and Bourbon. Valois kings ruled from 1328 to the 16th century.

In the late 15th century King Charles VIII (ruled 1483–1498) led France into a series of wars to gain the Kingdom of Naples in southern Italy. This was the start of decades of warfare between the Valois and the Hapsburgs, another leading European ruling family, who had rival dynastic claims in Italy.

### WAR IN ITALY

Francis I (ruled 1515–1547), the son of Charles de Valois-Orléans, was skilled in warfare. Within a year of becoming king, he had regained Milan in the Battle of Marignano (1515).

Francis made an unsuccessful bid to be elected Holy Roman emperor in 1519. The title went instead to the Hapsburg King Charles I of Spain (later known as Emperor Charles V), marking the start of a bitter rivalry between the two rulers that resulted in a series of wars.

The first war broke out in 1521, when Charles invaded northern Italy. The French lost Milan in 1522. Their

position in Italy was permanently weakened when Francis was captured by Hapsburg forces at the Battle of Pavia near Milan in 1525. His release was secured only after he agreed to hand over one-third of his territories and his two eldest sons to Charles. However, the surrendered lands rebelled against Charles, and in 1527 war was resumed. Little was to be gained by either side.

The wars with Spain had a disastrous effect on France's finances. The country also began to experience religious conflict. The number of

*Francis I of France is portrayed as a king of great splendor in this 16th-century painting. Francis was a Renaissance prince, in that he was a great patron of the arts and scholarship, as well as being skilled in warfare.*

Protestants grew as Martin Luther's reform ideas spread from Germany.

Francis had managed to reduce the pope's power over the church in France. He tolerated the French Protestants (called Huguenots) at first, but anti-Protestant feeling grew, and he began to repress them. Many fled abroad, including John Calvin, later a leading reformer. Based in Geneva, Calvin had a great influence on the Huguenots.

### RELIGIOUS CONFLICT

Francis died on March 31, 1547, and his second son, Henry II (ruled 1547–1559), became king. A strong Catholic, Henry tried to suppress the Huguenots while forming alliances with German Protestant princes against Charles V. Henry died unexpectedly in 1559, when he was fatally wounded in a tournament. Three of Henry's sons went on to become kings of France.

During his brief reign Francis II (ruled 1559–1560) was manipulated by his in-laws, the powerful Guise family. His successor, his brother Charles IX (ruled 1560–1574), was a pawn of their mother, Catherine de Médicis. At first Catherine tried to mediate between Catholics and Huguenots, but she was later implicated in the massacre of thousands of Huguenots in 1572.

Henry III (ruled 1574–1589) became king at a time when the great powers of Europe were struggling with bankruptcy and inflation, partly as a result of constant warfare. France had to devalue its currency to make sure its growing population did not starve.

Meanwhile, the cycle of violence in the religious wars continued. Catholic and Protestant rebel armies marauded through the countryside, with both armies a threat to the king. All parties favored assassination to remove their

*The marriage in 1533 of the future Henry II of France and Catherine de Médicis is conducted by Pope Clement VII. Henry was to bankrupt the royal government by continuing his father's policy of war against Charles V.*

# THE FRONDE

The Fronde consisted of two revolts in the years 1648 to 1653. The causes included anger at high taxes, the wish of the Parlement (a body with a largely judicial role) to curb the king's authority, and the ambitions of individual nobles. In the first rebellion, the Fronde of the Parlement, Parisians protested at government arrests of Parlement members. The prince of Condé led the royal army against the rebels in January 1649. The Fronde ended in March 1649 with the Peace of Rueil. Condé became overambitious, and Chief Minister Mazarin arrested him in January 1650, sparking provincial rebellions by Condé's noble followers, known as the Princes' Fronde. Condé was released, and Mazarin went into exile. However, Condé alienated his supporters by being arrogant and seizing Paris. Paris was recovered for the king, and Mazarin returned in October 1652, ending the Fronde. The instability caused by the Fronde prepared the way for Louis XIV's absolute rule, because the whole country came to view the king's party as the party of order.

opponents. Henry had the duke of Guise and his brother killed, and was in turn assassinated by a monk.

### THE RISE OF THE BOURBONS

Henry III's assassination ended the rule of the Valois. The new Bourbon king, Henry of Navarre, or Henry IV (ruled 1589–1610), was a Huguenot who converted to Catholicism in 1593. One of the most able kings of his time, Henry eventually ended the Wars of Religion by signing the Edict of Nantes in 1598. Under the edict Catholicism remained the state religion, but the Huguenots acquired religious freedom. Henry was a popular king who greatly improved France's finances. He was assassinated by a Catholic fanatic.

### CARDINAL RICHELIEU

Henry's son Louis XIII (ruled 1610–1643) was a boy when he became king, so initially his mother ruled. Louis took control in 1617. He appointed Cardinal Richelieu as chief minister. Richelieu laid the foundations for absolute rule by the French king. He reduced the power of the nobility by appointing officials (*intendants*) to govern the provinces on behalf of the crown. He also destroyed the Huguenots' political and military power in 1629 after capturing their stronghold, La Rochelle, in 1628. In the so-called Bourbon Reconstruction, Richelieu encouraged manufacturing and trade, but he also greatly increased taxes, thus planting the seeds of revolt.

Richelieu subsidized the Protestant states fighting against the Austrian Hapsburgs in the Thirty Years' War (1618–1648). In 1635 France also declared war on Hapsburg Spain. Supporting the Hapsburgs' enemies was a brilliant strategy that weakened the Hapsburgs as international rivals of

*In this painting by the French artist Pierre Courtillaud King Louis XIII (ruled 1610–1643) prepares to enter the rebel Huguenot stronghold of La Rochelle, which fell to state forces in 1628. Behind the king stands his chief minister, Cardinal Richelieu, who led the campaign against the Huguenots.*

France. A peace treaty with Spain was not signed until 1659.

## THE REIGN OF LOUIS XIV

Richelieu died in 1642 and Cardinal Mazarin took his place. During the reign of Louis XIV (ruled 1643–1715) Mazarin continued to impose high taxes to fund France's wars against Spain. This led to much discontent and a period of uprisings known as the Fronde (*see box left*). However, the wars resulted in France extending its borders, and also eventually in Louis's grandson Philip becoming king of Spain.

Louis believed that he had the right to govern without being answerable to anyone but God. He did all he could to reinforce his position as absolute monarch. After the chaos of the 16th century most French people were prepared to support absolutism for the sake of stability. Louis's reign was the longest and the most splendid in European history. The court at Versailles was famous for its luxury and extravagance. By 1715 France had become the leading European power.

*Henry IV takes part in the siege of Amiens in 1597, during the French Wars of Religion.*

# ENTERTAINING THE PEOPLE

Louis XIV was a great patron of the arts, and he supported many writers, musicians, artists, and architects during his long reign. Among them was the playwright Molière, who in 1661 wrote *Tartuffe*, satirizing the corruption of the French nobility. Called a demon in human form by the Catholic church, which threatened excommunication of those going to see the play, Molière was banned from putting on his plays in public. In 1667 his theater was closed by the government. However, within two years Louis XIV defied the church by granting a royal warrant that allowed Molière to perform his works again.

Cardinal Richelieu built a theater at his own expense, which he named the Palace Royale. In 1680 the French built the first national theater, the Comédie Française. The two theaters showed the works of other new playwrights, including Racine, who entertained with popular tragedies such as *Phaedra,* and Corneille. Very sophisticated methods of moving scenery were developed, enabling playwrights to be more imaginative. Although at first a recreation for the Paris nobility and middle class, the theater soon spread to many provincial towns, which were serviced by touring companies of actors.

# FREDERICK WILLIAM

**Frederick William (1620–1688), known as the Great Elector, was a leading German prince. After the Thirty Years' War (1618–1648) he unified the domains of the powerful Hohenzollern family, laying the foundations for the state of Prussia, the forerunner of modern Germany.**

The grandson of Elector John Sigismund of Brandenburg, a principality located in the northeast of the Holy Roman Empire, Frederick was born in 1620 during the Thirty Years' War (1618–1648) and spent most of his childhood in the fortress at Küstrin, on the Oder River in what is now Poland. At age 14 his parents, George William and Elizabeth Charlotte of the Palatinate, sent him to stay with relatives of his mother in the Netherlands, members of the ruling house of Orange. There he was educated at Leiden University. Frederick was very impressed by Dutch trade and commerce and their military and maritime prowess.

### FREDERICK'S RISE TO POWER

Frederick succeeded his father as elector of Brandenburg in 1640. He also inherited the Duchy of Prussia, on the Baltic coast of Poland, which had been jointly ruled with Brandenburg since 1618. He moved to Königsberg (now Kaliningrad), the capital of the Duchy of Prussia. There Frederick began his lifetime's work of trying to unify his scattered territories after the devastation caused to the region during decades of warfare. His first steps were to sign a truce with Sweden and

Russia, and reorganize Prussian bureaucracy, enabling the duchy to keep a well-trained professional army.

In 1646 Frederick married a Dutch princess, Louise Henriette of Orange,

*This engraving is a portrait of Frederick William, the Great Elector.*

hoping for Dutch military support, but it never materialized. In 1648, at the end of the Thirty Years' War, Frederick received lands that became important links to his western territories close to the French and Dutch borders.

### NORTHERN WARS

In 1655 Sweden invaded Poland, drawing Prussia into war. During the conflict Frederick initially fought with the Swedes; but when Sweden's fortunes declined, he allied with Austria and Poland. The allies drove the Swedes out of the region, and in 1660, by the Treaty of Oliva, Frederick gained complete control of Prussia.

Frederick's fledgling army had proved its worth in battle. Its strength was mostly due to funds raised by the new centralized tax system Frederick had created, rather than relying on intermittent financial support from the Holy Roman emperor.

In the 1670s northern Europe was once more engulfed in war as the French and Dutch fought over trade. Again Frederick switched sides, first allying himself with the Dutch against a French invasion, then fighting with the French. Next he adopted a policy of neutrality until his army joined forces with the Holy Roman emperor against the French in 1674. The next year the Swedes invaded Brandenburg, but Frederick's army defeated them and secured territory along the Baltic. However, at the end of the war in 1678 Frederick had to hand back some of his territories to the Swedes.

### FREDERICK'S LEGACY

During his lifetime Frederick rebuilt Brandenburg–Prussia and established it as an independent power, greatly improving its communications and leaving it with a strong and able army. Contemporary German folk songs described Frederick as the "Great Elector," who restored German pride and secured the motherland.

Frederick died in 1688, the year his nephew William III of Orange gained the English throne in the Glorious Revolution, changing the balance of power in Europe. His son Frederick I would create the Kingdom of Prussia in 1701, and his grandson Frederick II (the Great) would transform it into a major power in Europe.

*German engraver Matthaeus Merian's 1650 illustration shows the palace of the electors of Brandenburg in Berlin, in what is now Germany. The electors, including Frederick William, were princes who had the power to vote for new Holy Roman emperors.*

**SEE ALSO**

- Austria
- Germany
- Holy Roman Empire
- Northern Wars
- Poland–Lithuania
- Scandinavia
- Thirty Years' War

# FRENCH WARS OF RELIGION

A series of religious wars ravaged France between 1562 and 1598 as Protestants fought for freedom of worship against Catholics who were determined to stop the spread of Protestantism. Powerful aristocratic families tried to use the turbulent situation to gain more power.

Protestantism spread to France early in the 16th century, when Martin Luther's reform ideas reached Paris in 1519. At the time France was firmly Catholic. However, influential people—including the king's sister Margaret of Angoulême—began to join Protestant groups. Protestantism gained many followers from among minor landowners and also attracted people from poorer sections of society. French Protestants became known as Huguenots.

In 1534 King Francis I began to issue a series of repressive edicts against Huguenots, preventing them from worshiping freely. Yet Protestantism continued to spread. By 1561 more than 2,000 Protestant churches had been established in France.

### FIRST BLOOD

In 1560 Charles IX became king of France at age 10. Charles's mother, Catherine de Médicis, initially ruled on his behalf as regent. In 1562 Catherine attempted to defuse rising religious tension by issuing the Edict of January, allowing the Huguenots some rights to worship publicly. Catherine's edict led to an angry outburst from her political adversaries from the house of Guise, a powerful Catholic family. In one of the

worst atrocities of the period, on March 1, 1562, Duke Francis of Guise led a Catholic army into a Protestant church in Vassy and slaughtered more than 60 unarmed men, women, and children. The massacre sparked the first war of religion.

Guise forces took control of Paris while the Huguenots built up power and forces in the French provinces, with their headquarters at Orléans. During successive uprisings both the Catholics and the Huguenots suffered many losses. After the Battle of Dreux in 1562 both sides reached a settlement with the Peace of Amboise, permitting Protestants to practice their faith, but placing severe limitations on where religious services could be held.

*In this engraving by an unknown artist Huguenot churchgoers are massacred by Francis, duke of Guise, and his men at Vassy in 1562. The atrocity was one of the most brutal persecutions of Protestants before the Saint Bartholomew's Day Massacre in 1572.*

The peace did not last. In 1567 two Huguenot leaders, Louis I de Bourbon, Prince of Condé, and Admiral Gaspard de Coligny, attempted to overthrow the French royal family. This led to a second war that was settled at the Peace of Longjumeau in March 1568. By the end of the year, however, both sides had resumed fighting. Condé was killed at the Battle of Jarnac in 1569, and the Huguenots suffered a series of defeats before the Peace of Saint-Germain was reached in August 1570.

### PROTESTANTS MASSACRED

Catherine de Médicis was determined to protect Charles's throne. She allied with the Guise family in an attempt to assassinate Coligny, but the plot failed. As the Peace of Longjumeau faltered, Catherine persuaded the king to crush the Huguenots or risk facing a Protestant rebellion.

On August 23, 1572, the eve of the feast of Saint Bartholomew, many Huguenots were gathered in Paris to celebrate the wedding of the leading Huguenot Henry of Navarre, Condé's nephew, to Catherine's daughter Margaret of Valois. On Charles's orders soldiers killed Coligny and other Huguenot leaders. Then the situation got out of hand—an estimated 3,000 Huguenots were slaughtered in Paris, and the killing spread to the provinces. Over three days more than 20,000 Huguenots were killed across France, perhaps as many as 70,000. Protestants across Europe were horrified. In Rome Pope Gregory XIII celebrated the massacre as a victory for Catholicism.

France quickly descended into another bloody war. After the death of Charles IX in 1575 Henry III became king. The next year the Peace of Monsieur brought a brief end to fighting, when Henry signed the Edict of Beaulieu and gave Protestants the freedom to worship outside Paris. Renewed fighting in 1577 was brought to a close by the Peace of Bergerac, and between 1577 and 1584 France was relatively peaceful.

In 1584, however, the king's brother Francis died. The next in line to the throne was now the king's cousin, the Protestant Henry of Navarre. Some years before, in 1576, the Guise family had formed the anti-Protestant Catholic League, a group devoted to preventing Henry of Navarre gaining the throne. War now broke out once

*This contemporary painting shows a procession of the anti-Protestant Catholic League through the Place de Gréve in Paris, France, in 1590.*

again, with King Philip II of Spain supporting the Catholic League. Between 1585 and 1589 both sides suffered heavy losses. The duke of Guise and his brother were murdered, and in 1589 the king himself was assassinated. By now the Catholic League controlled France; and although Henry of Navarre was next in line to the throne, Catholics forced him to flee to the south of the country. Over the next five years Henry fought to claim the French throne, winning two decisive victories at Arques in 1589 and Ivry in 1590. In 1594 Henry is famously reported to have said, "Paris is worth a Mass," and at last entered Paris, after renouncing Protestantism and joining the Catholic church. That same year he was crowned king of France. The Catholic League was dissolved two years later.

### MAKING THE PEACE

Henry realized that the continuous wars had to stop for France to achieve stability. In 1598 he signed the Edict of Nantes. The edict established France as a Catholic nation but gave the Huguenots new rights, including the right to worship in public, the right to attend schools and universities, and the right to occupy public offices and serve in local governments and councils. The Edict of Nantes finally brought the Wars of Religion to a close and brought a degree of religious and financial stability to France that it had not experienced for nearly 40 years.

*Henry of Navarre, or Henry IV (ruled 1589–1610), rides into Paris in 1594 after being crowned in the Cathedral of Chartres, in this contemporary painting. For over five years he fought Catholic forces to reclaim his throne.*

## CONTINUING PERSECUTION

Although the Wars of Religion ended in 1598, religious persecution would blight French life for years to come. In 1610 Henry IV was murdered, and the young Louis XIII became king. Under his chief minister, Cardinal Richelieu, the persecution of Protestants resumed.

The French army crushed Huguenot towns and cities throughout France, and Protestants lost their jobs, were imprisoned, or even killed. Later in the 17th century, during the reign of Louis XIV (ruled 1643–1715), the persecution intensified. Louis rejected the Edict of Nantes in 1685; Protestant churches and books were burned, and hundreds of Protestants were executed. Many were forced to convert to Catholicism. More than 400,000 French Protestants fled abroad. Only with the Edict of Tolerance signed more than 100 years later were French Protestants given back some of their religious and civil rights.

### SEE ALSO

- Calvin, John
- Catherine de Médicis
- Catholic church
- France
- Henry of Navarre
- Huguenots
- Reformation

# FUGGER FAMILY

The Fuggers were a family of German merchants and bankers who built one of the most prosperous European financial empires in the 16th century. They became the personal bankers to the Hapsburgs and the Holy Roman Empire.

The Fugger family was descended from Johannes Fugger (1348–1409), a linen weaver who moved to the southern German town of Augsburg in 1367. His descendants built up the family fortune by trading textiles and luxuries such as silks, gems, spices, and slaves. From the late 1400s the Fuggers were granted a lucrative monopoly on mining and trading lead, silver, copper, and mercury by successive Holy Roman emperors in places such as Bohemia and Hungary in central Europe. The Fuggers' wealth was so great that they acted as bankers to various European rulers and princes.

### A BANKING EMPIRE

The Fugger family reached the height of its glory under Jakob Fugger II (1459–1525), also known as "Jakob the Rich." Under Jakob the family firm became primarily a banking house, with branches in the Netherlands, Italy, and Spain. It concentrated on international loans to governments and rulers. Jakob organized enormous loans for the Hapsburg Holy Roman Emperor Maximilian I (1493–1519). By the end of his life Maximilian was so deeply in debt to Jakob that he had to pawn the royal jewels. Jakob also provided loans

to Maximilian's grandson, Charles V, and helped secure his election as Holy Roman emperor in 1519 by bribing the electors. The Fuggers reaped handsome profits from their connections with the Hapsburg family.

At the time of Jakob's death in 1525 the Fuggers were the most influential

*A 16th-century illustration showing Jakob Fugger II (right) in his office. Jakob built up the hugely powerful Fugger business empire.*

*These houses for poorer citizens of Augsburg were built and financed by the Fugger family. Jakob Fugger II began this charitable housing project, known as the Fuggerei, around 1516 to provide homes for Catholic artisans and laborers.*

bankers in Europe. Their business network reached from Hungary and Poland to Spain and Portugal, from Antwerp to Naples, and across the Indian Ocean. Their firm owned extensive real estate, merchant fleets, and palaces. They were the richest family in Europe, were generous supporters of the Catholic church and the arts, and gave money to charitable projects. Under Jakob's nephew and successor, Anton (1493–1560), the Fuggers' business continued to flourish. By the 1560s, however, the family's fortunes had taken a turn for the worse. The flood of gold and silver from new mines in America ended the central European mining boom, and the Hapsburg King Philip II of Spain (ruled 1556–1598) failed to repay huge loans the bank had made him. The Fugger family business continued into the 17th century but never regained the status it had previously enjoyed.

**SEE ALSO**

- Banks and banking
- Charles V
- Hapsburg family
- Holy Roman Empire
- Mining
- Taxes and government finances
- Trade

## NEWS FROM ENGLAND

Between 1568 and 1604 the Fugger family had agents all over Europe who gathered information about anything that affected trade or might be of relevance to the family's business interests. They sent this information back to the bank in thousands of letters, like this one, which was written in Antwerp on September 6, 1586:

*"London letters recently received announce that Drake the pirate [Francis Drake] has arrived in London from India with 50 to 60 ships. He is said to have brought great wealth with him, but the ships are not yet unloaded. They also write of an important case of treason against the Queen's life [Queen Elizabeth I of England]. Monsieur de Guise had arranged with certain nobles to come to England, but the conspiracy was discovered and some 60 persons, many of high birth, have been imprisoned. A man who came here from England recently says that this plot took place before his departure from London, and that an Englishman shot at the Queen. But before he fired, the bullet, without his noticing it, fell out of the pistol, so he missed her. Nevertheless the Queen's hair seems to have been singed. The Earl of Leicester [whom Elizabeth put in charge of English troops sent to the Netherlands to support the Dutch revolt against their Spanish overlords] is stated to have pitched his camp between Utrecht and Amersfoort."*

# GALILEO GALILEI

The Italian mathematician, astronomer, and natural philosopher Galileo Galilei (1564–1642) was one of the founders of the modern scientific revolution. He made important discoveries in astronomy, physics, and the study of motion.

Galileo was born in Pisa, Italy. He studied at the city's university, where he became a professor of mathematics at age 25. In 1592 Galileo moved to Padua university, where he was based until 1610. His time at Padua was very fruitful. He studied the motion of pendulums and developed his ideas about mechanics, or the science of the motion of objects under the action of natural forces. He formulated his law that all falling objects speed up at the same rate. Galileo also took a sharp interest in the heliocentric system proposed by the Polish astronomer Nicolaus Copernicus (1473–1543). This theory held that the earth moves around the sun, as opposed to the older Ptolemaic idea that the earth is stationary and that the sun and the planets revolve around it.

## DEVELOPMENTS IN ASTRONOMY

In about 1608 Galileo began to take a serious interest in astronomy, the area of study for which he is now best known. On hearing about the invention of the telescope in the Netherlands, he quickly developed his own version of the instrument. He gradually improved his design so that it could magnify

objects 33 times more than if seen by the unaided eye. When Galileo turned his telescope to the skies, he saw things that contradicted beliefs that had been held for centuries. He observed that the moon did not have a smooth surface but was crinkled with valleys and mountains, and that the Milky Way was not a misty white stream but masses of individual stars. He also discovered that the planet Jupiter had four satellites, or moons, orbiting it.

Galileo published his discoveries in *The Starry Messenger* (1610), a book in which he made clear his support for the Copernican model of the universe. Over the following years his ideas were attacked by other professors, who clung

*A 19th-century copy of a portrait of Galileo painted by Justus Sustermans in about 1636. The painting shows Galileo in his seventies, near the end of a long career in which his discoveries helped shape modern science but also roused the opposition of the Catholic church.*

# GALILEO'S TRIAL

After publication of Galileo's book *Dialogue Concerning the Two Chief World Systems* (1632) the Catholic church realized that Galileo supported Copernicus's heliocentric system, which it considered to be heretical. Pope Urban VIII ordered the printing of the book to be halted while an investigation took place. In September 1632 Galileo was summoned to Rome, and in the following year he was put on trial by the Roman Inquisition. Threatened with torture if he did not disown his support of Copernicus's ideas, Galileo was compelled to kneel in front of church officials and recant his views. There is a story that after doing so he whispered, "E pur si muove" ("And yet it [the earth] moves"), although there is no evidence to support this. Despite recanting, Galileo was sentenced to life imprisonment, a sentence later reduced to house arrest. His *Dialogue* was put on the church's Index of Prohibited Books.

*This 19th-century painting shows Galileo being tried by the church court of the Inquisition in Rome in 1633.*

to traditional ideas, and by members of the church, for whom Copernicus's theories were heretical because they seemed to contradict the Bible.

Early in 1616 Cardinal Robert Bellarmine commanded Galileo not to "hold or defend" the concept that the earth moves around the sun. Eight years later Galileo obtained permission from the pope to write about the Ptolemaic and Copernican views of the universe, as long as he treated the latter merely as a theory rather than truth. The result was his book *Dialogue Concerning the Two Chief World Systems*, published in 1632. However, Galileo's obvious bias toward the Copernican system led to his trial in a church court (*see box*). Afterward, despite poor health and blindness, he continued to work and produced a book on the science of motion and the strength of materials: *Discourses Concerning Two New Sciences* (1638). Galileo died in 1642.

**SEE ALSO**

- Astronomy
- Copernicus, Nicolaus
- Inventions and inventors
- Science

# GARDEN DESIGN

From 1500 most peasants' dwellings, monasteries, and kings' palaces had gardens of varying sizes to provide vegetables and fruit. The homes of the middle and upper classes also had ornamental gardens, which became increasingly grand and elaborate from the mid-15th century.

New ideas about gardens reflected broader changes in society. In the Middle Ages nobles and kings had had to fortify their homes against attack. This necessity and a fear of the untamed wilderness meant that their gardens were often enclosed and protected from the outside world by walls. From the 15th century the need to fortify homes began to lessen, and attitudes toward the natural world changed. Gardens began to open out and embrace views of the landscape beyond.

Growing knowledge about the natural world and exploration of new lands also brought changes. New species of trees, shrubs, and flowers were introduced and cultivated, including lilacs, hyacinths, crocuses, and tulips. These plants were studied and classified in the botanical gardens set up by universities from the mid-1500s.

## ITALIAN GARDENS

New attitudes to garden design were most evident in Italian gardens, which from the mid-15th century began to reflect Renaissance interest in classical (ancient Greek and Roman) art and ideas. To display their status, many powerful men ordered grand new houses and palaces designed in styles based on those of antiquity. Soon they began to order gardens to match.

While Italian Renaissance gardens varied widely, they typically included many built elements, such as paving, walls, statues, benches, grottoes (artificial caves), and water features, particularly fountains. Flowers were usually planted in beds divided into geometrical shapes by trimmed hedges of box or herbs. Evergreens such as cypress, ilex, laurel, and ivy were also

*Water cascades from the Fontana dell'Ovato, one of the many fountains in the 16th-century gardens of the Villa d'Este at Tivoli, Italy.*

popular. The description of a villa and its garden by Roman writer Pliny the Younger (about 62–113 A.D.) inspired many 16th-century gardens, including that at the Villa d'Este in Tivoli, near Rome. This garden, designed by Pirro Ligorio (about 1500–1583), comprised many water features and fountains laid out on a steeply terraced hill.

## FRENCH GARDENS

In the 17th century France became the center of advances in garden design. The country had long involved itself in Italian affairs and been influenced by Italian culture. French courtiers and royalty came to regard Italian-style gardens as the height of fashion.

In France the formality and symmetry of Italian gardens was developed on a huge scale. Gardens were designed around a central axis and spread over vast areas. Lesser gardens were often contained within wooded enclosures to either side of the main axis and were intended for the staging of dramatic spectacles. Flower beds enclosed by small trimmed hedges and separated by networks of paths (parterres) spread over large areas like outdoor carpets. Often these elaborate patterns were made from colored stones and sand rather than plants. Statues, urns, and elaborate fountains provided focal points throughout the grounds.

French courtiers and kings ordered Italian-inspired designs to complement their new castles in the Loire Valley and around Paris. One of the finest of these gardens was laid out for Nicholas Fouquet, minister of finance to Louis XIV, at Vaux-le-Vicomte (finished in 1661). It was the work of the most brilliant garden designer of the time, André Le Nôtre (1613–1700). Louis soon employed Le Nôtre to design the magnificent grounds of his royal palaces, most famously Versailles, which became the model for many great European gardens in the 1700s.

*People promenade in the gardens of the Château Saint-Cloud, France, in this 17th-century print. Created by André Le Nôtre, the gardens show the formality, symmetry, and large scale popular in French garden design in the 17th century.*

SEE ALSO
- Architecture
- Botany
- Capitalism
- Environment
- Renaissance
- Versailles

# GENEVA

**In the 16th century the Swiss city-state of Geneva was one of the most influential centers of the Reformation. It became Protestant in the 1530s and under the leadership of the reformer and theologian John Calvin (1509–1564) developed a new type of church and government.**

Geneva is situated at a key crossroads in the Alps, the mountainous barrier that separates northern Europe from the Italian Peninsula. The city's strategic position contributed to its growth and prosperity in the Middle Ages. The dukes of Savoy annexed Geneva in the 13th century. Geneva's authorities succeeded in freeing themselves from Savoy rule in the early 16th century, but the dukes continued to exercise influence in the city through their support of the bishop of Geneva.

### ACHIEVING INDEPENDENCE

By the 1530s the Reformation had taken hold in Germany and some parts of Switzerland. The religious and political changes it brought offered Geneva an alternative to traditional Savoy influence. In 1533 the Genevans dissolved the bishopric of Geneva. Two years later they declared their city a republic. However, when the duke of Savoy threatened invasion, Geneva was forced to ally itself to the Protestant Swiss canton (state) of Bern. The alliance was sealed by religion, and in 1536 Geneva became Protestant. In December 1602 the then duke of Savoy, Charles Emmanuel, failed in his attempt to conquer the city.

Geneva grew in the 16th century, when thousands of Protestants fled there to escape persecution in Catholic countries such as Italy and France.

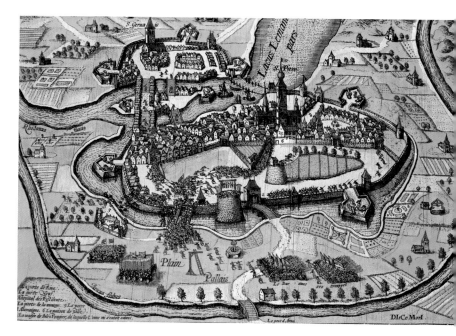

Many also fled there from England in the reign of Mary I (ruled 1553–1558), when Catholicism was reintroduced and Protestantism bloodily suppressed.

### CENTER OF REFORM

Many of the refugees were skilled professionals and craftsmen, and they contributed to Geneva's development as a center for clockmaking, banking, and cloth manufacture. The most influential of these newcomers was the French reformer John Calvin.

Calvin had studied humanities and law at the French universities of Paris and Orléans. By the early 1530s he had adopted Protestant ideas and was writing extensively about religion. In 1536 he published his most influential

*A 17th-century print shows the duke of Savoy's troops scaling Geneva's city walls on December 11, 1602. The assault was successfully beaten back, a victory that is still celebrated in Geneva in the Festival of the Escalade, or the scaling of the walls.*

work, *Institutes of the Christian Religion.* This was a clear statement of his Protestant beliefs.

### CALVIN'S CHRISTIAN STATE

The French Protestant reformer Guillaume Farel, who was preaching in Geneva, persuaded Calvin to help him in 1536. By the following year Calvin had developed a clear program for putting into practice the ideas he had laid out in his *Institutes.* However, the council—the city's ruling body—refused to accept some elements of the reformed faith and the changes they necessitated in the way the city and church were run. As a result, Farel and Calvin were forced to leave Geneva in 1638. Three years later, when it became apparent that a strong leader was needed to establish Protestantism in the city, Calvin was invited back.

In 1541 the council implemented the measures that Calvin laid out for the creation of a Christian state in his *Ecclesiastical Ordinances* (1541). All townspeople were given religious education, and the church was restructured. Pastors and teachers preached and explained the Bible, elders administered the church, and deacons carried out charitable work. An organization called a consistory ensured that all aspects of life in Geneva conformed to God's law.

### OPPOSITION TO CALVIN

Some people objected to Calvin's ideas: The so-called Libertine Party staged an unsuccessful uprising in 1555. From then on the Calvinist model of Protestantism established in Geneva became hugely influential in Europe and North America. Calvinism inspired several new Christian denominations, including the Dutch Reformed and the Presbyterian churches. After Calvin died in 1564, Geneva continued to attract Protestants from around the world, particularly Calvinists.

*This painting shows John Calvin addressing the council of Geneva in the 1540s. He transformed the way the church and state were run in Geneva, and made the city one of the major centers of Protestantism in the 16th century.*

SEE ALSO

- Calvin, John
- Government, systems of
- Luther, Martin
- Reformation
- Switzerland
- Zwingli, Huldrych

# GERMANY

**In 1500, on the eve of the Reformation, Germany was a patchwork of more than 300 states ruled by princes, bishops, and lords. Until the 1700s most of these states were loosely organized in the Holy Roman Empire, under an emperor who was elected by the more powerful rulers.**

The German states differed greatly in size and power. Those whose rulers elected the Holy Roman emperor were most powerful. Next were the secular and ecclesiastical states. They were surrounded by the territories of lesser princes and more than 100 counts, 70 bishoprics, and 66 free and imperial cities. The remaining states were ruled by 2,000 imperial knights, each based in his own castle and controlling the peasants living on the surrounding lands. While many states recognized the advantages of unification to improve defense and trade, they could rarely agree on how it would be best achieved.

### RELIGIOUS DISPUTES

Before the Reformation the Catholic church was Germany's main unifying force. However, in 1517 the reformer Martin Luther delivered his 95 Theses, outlining problems in the church. The resulting fervor divided Germany. North Germans flocked to the Protestant banner, while southerners remained loyal to the Catholic faith. Charles V, the Catholic Holy Roman emperor from 1519 to 1556, constantly clashed with Protestant north German princes.

The emperor and the princes eventually reached an agreement in 1555 with the Peace of Augsburg. The treaty established the principle of *cuius regio, eius religio* ("he who rules the territory determines its religion"),

which gave each prince the right to choose the religion his subjects should follow. Scarred by the Peasants' Revolt in 1525 (*see box p. 22*), the mass of German peasants, whose religion was now locally dictated, simply switched between Lutheran and Catholic forms of worship as their lords decreed.

### GERMANY'S ECONOMY

The German states suffered prolonged economic depression throughout the late 16th century. The north German Hanseatic League, an alliance of trading towns, had once dominated trade in the Baltic and North seas but could no longer compete against Dutch, Danish, and English merchants.

Southern Germany was also suffering. At the beginning of the 16th century its cities had been enterprising and wealthy, but political disputes had caused the economy to decline. As each

*A 1557 woodcut of the Protestant reformer Martin Luther at the Diet of Worms in 1521. The Holy Roman Emperor Charles V (seated, with crown) presided over the diet and afterward declared Luther an outlaw.*

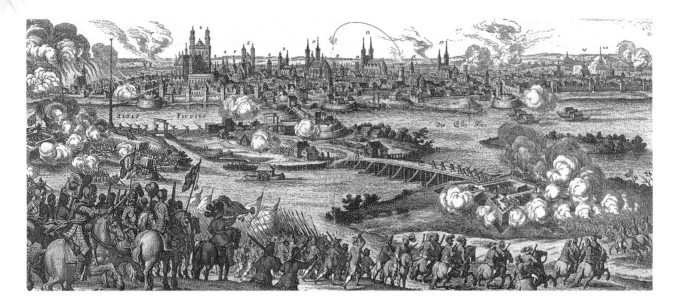

prince tried to increase his wealth and power through levying local taxes, trade was stifled and manufacturing output fell. Entrepreneurs lost their fortunes, and German cities went into decline.

### WAR AND DIVISION

The Thirty Years' War (1618–1648), a conflict that engaged most of Europe, caused widespread devastation in Germany and ruined the economy. Perhaps one-third of the German population died during the conflict.

The Peace of Westphalia (1648) officially concluded the war and set new guidelines for religious toleration. However, significant division remained between Protestants and Catholics. The peace recognized the sovereign, independent authority of the German princes, dramatically undermining the authority of the Holy Roman emperor.

In the absence of Hapsburg authority neighboring France and Sweden began to encroach on the German states, frequently interfering in local German affairs. By the end of the 17th century the influence of the Holy Roman emperor and the papacy in Germany had been greatly reduced.

*This engraving by Mattheaus Merian shows the siege of the city of Magdeburg in central Germany in 1631 during the Thirty Years' War. Hapsburg imperial forces sacked it and massacred many of the inhabitants.*

## THE PEASANTS' REVOLT

In the early 16th century demands from landlords for greater labor services and higher rents made life difficult for peasants. There were uprisings in 1524; then in 1525 a major revolt began, which eventually involved around 250,000 people. The peasants released the "Twelve Articles," a list of both social demands (such as for fair rents), and also religious ones that were heavily influenced by the ideas of Martin Luther. They insisted that from then on ministers should be elected by the whole congregation, and that the Holy Gospel should be taught in a pure and simple form. Luther, however, disagreed with the militant stance of the rebels and disowned them. The poorly armed peasant army was defeated at the Battle of Frankenhausen in May 1525. After the battle resistance movements across the region collapsed. As the landlords regained control in the affected areas, harsh punishments were meted out; about 100,000 peasants were executed.

**SEE ALSO**

- Charles V
- Counter Reformation
- Hapsburg family
- Holy Roman Empire
- Luther, Martin
- Reformation
- Thirty Years' War

# GLORIOUS REVOLUTION

In the Glorious Revolution of 1688 King James II of England and Scotland was deposed in favor of his daughter Mary and her husband, Prince William III of Orange, stadtholder of the Netherlands. This is also known as the Bloodless Revolution since there was little violence.

James II became king of England and Scotland in 1685, on the death of his elder brother Charles II. A staunch Catholic, he quickly aroused the hostility of many of his powerful Protestant subjects by appointing Catholics to important positions in the government and army. He did so in defiance of the Test Act of 1673, which barred them from such posts.

In 1687 James issued a Declaration of Indulgence, which granted full freedom of worship to all Christians and a general suspension of laws against Catholics and Nonconformists (Protestants who were not members of the Church of England). When Charles II had attempted similar measures, Parliament had declared them illegal. In an effort to avoid this happening again, James suspended Parliament and announced plans to replace it with another that would do his bidding. The new body was due to be convened in November 1688.

Meanwhile James issued a second Declaration of Indulgence and ordered it to be announced in every church in the country on two successive Sundays in April 1688. When the Archbishop of Canterbury, head of the Church of England, and six bishops petitioned the

*William of Orange enters London on December 18, 1688, after King James II had fled. William had agreed to lead an expedition to England against James, partly because he wanted to secure English support for the Dutch against the French.*

*In this engraving, members of Parliament offer the crown of England to William and Mary in the banqueting hall of Whitehall Palace on February 13, 1689. The monarchs' coronation took place in April.*

king to withdraw his decree, James had them arrested and put on trial. They were acquitted by a jury.

In June 1688 James had a son by his second wife, the Catholic Mary of Modena. Faced with the prospect of future Catholic monarchs, James's opponents invited his elder daughter, Mary, and her husband, the Protestant Prince William of Orange, to England.

William agreed, arguing that James should acknowledge Mary's right to succeed him. On November 5 William and 20,000 troops landed in southwest England without opposition. James sent 40,000 men to meet the invasion force but suffered a nervous breakdown himself and remained in London. Without the king at its head James's army surrendered to William. On December 10 James fled to France.

### A NEW CONSTITUTION

By leaving the country, James in effect abdicated. The crown was offered jointly to William and Mary in early 1689, and they accepted. The new monarchs assented to the Bill of Rights, which laid the foundations for a new English constitution, shifting power in England from the monarch to Parliament. The bill stated that Parliament had to meet frequently, there should be freedom of speech in Parliament, and no future English monarch could be Catholic. The monarch could no longer suspend or dispense with laws, raise taxes, or keep a standing army during peacetime without Parliament's consent.

In 1690 James tried to recapture the throne, but William defeated him at the Battle of the Boyne in Ireland, and James returned to France.

Other laws, which stated that Parliament should meet every three years and limited the time a monarch could rule by martial law, consolidated the new settlement. The Toleration Act granted Nonconformist Protestants freedom of worship, but Catholics continued to be repressed. In 1694 an act of Parliament provided for the creation of the Bank of England, a joint stock venture that raised funds for Williams's war against France and helped the monarch manage the national debt.

SEE ALSO

- England
- English Reformation
- Stuart family
- William of Orange

# GOVERNMENT, SYSTEMS OF

The period between 1500 and 1700 was a time of transition for European systems of government. The role of the nobles in government declined. In some states the monarch moved toward absolutism, while in others a representative assembly became more powerful.

In Europe during the Middle Ages there were few governments as we know them today. Individuals owed loyalty to other individuals rather than to a state or nation, and few written laws were enforced to regulate people's conduct. People believed that God had ordained the social and political order, and so the role of the church in life was very important.

### TYPES OF GOVERNMENT

There were many different types of government: cities ruled by archbishops appointed by the pope; provinces ruled by independent dukes who barely acknowledged a king; trading towns whose merchants elected their own rulers. These independent institutions had freedoms and privileges that they were very unwilling to give up.

There were powerful kings and emperors in the Middle Ages, but they always had to take account of two powerful groups: The leading nobles who controlled large areas had their own fortified castles and could raise armies of followers, and the towns and cities that had grown rich through trade, and whose money became increasingly important.

During the 16th and 17th centuries things did not change much for many

*The Parliament of England meets in 1584, during the reign of Elizabeth I. Parliament had been summoned every year between 1529 and 1559, when its support was needed to establish the new Church of England in the English Reformation. Later in Elizabeth's reign, however, Parliament met far less frequently.*

people living in the countryside. Their lives were governed by the rhythm of the changing seasons and the weather, the religious system that defined their social lives and feast days, and the local lord who dominated their village, and to whom they often had to give a large part of their farm produce. Any representatives of central government were likely to cause trouble—such as by

# LEVELLERS AND DIGGERS

During the English Civil War (1642–1648) many groups emerged with differing ideas on how their country should be governed. One group was the Levellers. From 1645 they voiced demands for a number of reforms, including the abolition of the monarchy and House of Lords, the extension of the right to vote to all men except servants, and the abolition of a state church and tithes (an annual payment to the church). Their support came from the poorer and middle-ranking people in London and southern England. They drew up a draft constitution, and in 1647 it was debated at Putney in London by leaders of the New Model Army, which had secured victory over the Royalists in the Civil War. The Levellers' ideas were not accepted, and in 1649 they were repressed following mutinies within the army.

Holding even more radical ideas than the Levellers were the Diggers. In 1649, under the leadership of Gerrard Winstanley, the Diggers began communal cultivation of former crown and common land at Saint George's Hill near London. By the spring of 1650 they had been destroyed by a combination of local and army opposition.

*John Lilburne, a political agitator and leader of the Levellers, appeals to a crowd as he stands at a pillory. He was imprisoned many times, but in 1649 he was tried for sedition and acquitted.*

this period, however, especially in the larger European states. The most basic change was that the power of the senior nobles was declining, partly because new technology such as cannons meant that their castles were out of date. In contrast, towns and cities grew more important since money was now essential for paying for weapons and hiring professional soldiers to fight. In addition, the clashes over religion meant that central government interfered in ordinary people's lives more than ever before across Europe.

There were two major trends in government during this period: toward more control being vested in a single ruler (absolutism) and toward more control being given to assemblies of representatives, normally of the landowning classes. Sometimes these processes went together.

## GROWTH OF ABSOLUTISM

Absolutism was a natural outcome once the power of the nobles began to decline. All rulers wanted to be able to extend their control over their subjects and to be able to raise more money. The great states of Europe all had experience of absolute rule. In Spain, for example, after the unification of the country in 1492 Ferdinand of Aragon and Isabella of Castile ruled jointly and reduced the power of the old nobility by replacing the traditional council of nobles with people they appointed themselves. But absolutism also clashed with local interests. When Holy Roman Emperor Charles V was king of Spain, he tried to raise more money from Spanish towns. In response they revolted and were supported by the nobility. The result was that the kings of Spain found it difficult to raise money during the rest of the century.

The greatest success of absolutism came in France in the 17th century.

wanting to conscript men into the army. Then, too, many states barely changed in their form of government, for example, the cantons of Switzerland or city-states such as Geneva or Venice.

There were important changes in the government of many areas during

Two important chief ministers, Cardinal Richelieu (served 1624–1642) and Cardinal Mazarin (served 1643–1661), prepared the ground by asserting central religious and political control over all of France. Then King Louis XIV, for whom Mazarin had acted as regent until 1661, set up a system of absolute government that was widely admired across Europe.

Louis XIV used his own governors, or *intendants*, to rule the French provinces rather than rely on the old nobility and was able to run the

## GOVERNMENT IN THE OTTOMAN EMPIRE

The head of government in the Turkish Ottoman Empire was the sultan, an absolute monarch who officially combined the three roles of war leader, law-giver, and Muslim official. The empire was always engaged in conquest, and until the late 17th century the sultan spent several months each year campaigning with his army. There was often no time to attend to the administration of the empire, which became the responsibility of four officials appointed by the sultan: the grand vizier, the judge advocate, the minister of finance, and the secretary of state. The grand vizier was by far the most powerful, with responsibilities that included foreign policy and military organization.

The position of sultan was hereditary within the Ottoman ruling house. However, because under Muslim law there was no principle of inheritance by the eldest son, several sons might pursue competing claims to the throne. The problem was partly solved by allowing each new sultan to execute all his brothers and their male children.

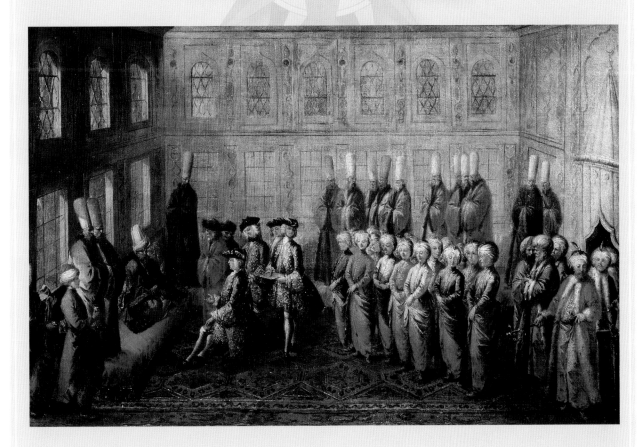

*The Ottoman Grand Vizier Ahmed Köprülü meets the French ambassador in Istanbul, Turkey, in 1670. Köprülü, who was of Albanian origin, succeeded his father as grand vizier and was much involved in military campaigns.*

country as he pleased. He managed to raise enough money to maintain a large standing army. France was recognized as the major power in Europe.

## REPRESENTATIVE ASSEMBLIES

The second major trend was toward more representation for some of the population of a country. This often happened in reaction to attempts to impose absolutism. In what is now the Netherlands, for example, the population revolted in 1566 against attempts by their ruler King Philip II of Spain to reduce the privileges of the towns and to stamp out Protestantism. The resulting war of independence did not finally end until 1648 and left a nation in which property owners had a great say in the government.

The reaction against absolutism was most clearly seen in England, where attempts to rule without consulting a representative assembly by Charles I in the 1630s and then by his son James II in the 1680s led to revolution and the king being deposed. The Glorious Revolution of 1688 led to a settlement in which the powers of the representative assembly, the Parliament, were declared to be greater than those of the monarchy. This was a critical step on the road to modern democracy.

Sometimes, however, representative assemblies gained power by being given it by rulers. The English Parliament, for example, became important during the 16th century because Henry VIII and later monarchs called it often and used it to help them push through religious changes and to raise taxes. Similarly, in Sweden in the early 17th century King Gustavus Adolphus created a representative body to gain support for his reforms.

These representative assemblies were not like modern legislatures, however. For a start, there was no voting by a

majority of inhabitants—just by a few property owners (if there was voting at all). There were some revolutionaries who dared demand greater freedoms, but this was considered very dangerous.

## SUPPRESSING RADICAL IDEAS

In Germany the peasants of the 1520s who wanted some political influence and the radical Protestants known as Anabaptists later in the century were put down by force. In the 1640s during the revolutionary period in England ideas of democracy gained a hold, especially among groups such as the Levellers and Diggers (*see box p. 26*), but they were never in a position to take power.

*Louis XIV of France, portrayed here in 1701, was renowned as an absolute monarch.*

SEE ALSO

- English Revolution
- France
- Glorious Revolution
- Monarchy and absolutism
- Ottoman Empire
- Popular rebellions
- Social order

# EL GRECO

The painter El Greco (1541–1614) had a highly original style of painting. He imbued his religious subjects with an intense spirituality conveyed through vigorous brushwork, distorted forms, bright colors, and dramatic light effects.

El Greco (the Greek) was born Doménikos Theotokopoulous in Candia on the Greek island of Crete. Not much is known about his early life. Scholars think that he trained as a painter of religious images called icons in either a monastery or a painter's studio. Around 1566 he left Crete to study in Venice, which at the time controlled the island.

In Italy El Greco saw the work of the great Renaissance artists. In particular he was influenced by the paintings of the Venetian artist Titian (about 1488–1576). After El Greco moved to Rome in 1570, he admired the powerful and expressive way that Michelangelo (1475–1564) portrayed the human figure.

In 1588 El Greco moved to Spain, probably in search of the patronage of King Philip II (ruled 1556–1598). In the event, he received few commissions from the king. He set up a successful workshop in Toledo, however, just outside Madrid, where he specialized in altarpieces and religious paintings. He also produced portraits. One of his most famous paintings is *Burial of the Count of Orgaz* (1586). It depicts a miracle relating to the Spanish noble Don Gonzales Ruiz, who died in the

14th century. Other nobles around the count mourn his death. Above the burial scene El Greco shows heaven as a mass of swirling forms, saints, and angels, lit by a pale, otherworldly glow.

Some commentators have tried to account for El Greco's unusual style by proposing that he was insane or that he had problems with his eyesight. Instead, his style seems to be inspired by Byzantine mosaics, his early training in Crete painting religious icons, and his experience with Italian art. His dynamic work, shaped by the ideas of the Counter Reformation, provides a visual counterpart to the spiritual writings of Ignatius of Loyola and Teresa of Avila.

*In El Greco's* **Burial of the Count of Orgaz** *(1586) Saints Augustine and Stephen lower the count's body into a grave, while above an angel guides his soul to heaven.*

SEE ALSO

- Counter Reformation
- Painting
- Spain
- Titian

# GUILDS AND CRAFTS

**Artisans and craftspeople formed the backbone of commercial development in Europe between 1500 and 1700. Most banded together in guilds that regulated features of their trade, such as apprenticeships, wages, and the quality and kind of work that members would perform.**

Craft guilds were associations of workers who performed the same trade or craft, such as weavers, silversmiths, or armorers. Merchants, bankers, and notaries, who were all members of the urban elite, also formed guilds that played an important role in city politics.

Guilds played a very important part in urban life. People who moved to towns or cities from the countryside could often feel isolated, having grown up in a village where they knew everyone. Guilds offered a sense of community for people living in the city. Guild members often worked and lived in the same area and went to the same parish church, paid into a fund for their burial services, appealed to the guild master in trade disputes, and relied on him to represent their trade in city government.

## RIGHTS AND RULES
Guild membership conveyed both rights and responsibilities. Guild members paid dues so that the guild could provide old age and disability pensions and pensions for the widows of its members. If a guild member was accused of a crime, the guild might even fund part of his legal defense. In return, guild members were expected to

follow guild rules concerning the prices they could charge for their work, the number of days a week they could work, and the kind and quality of goods they could produce. Working out of hours, skimping on materials, or prices that undercut other guildsmen were not allowed and were grounds for expulsion from the guild. Without guild membership a craftsman did not have the right to work in the city and could be driven out.

## A CRAFTSMAN AND HIS GUILD
The relationship between craftsmen and their guild began when young people became apprenticed to a

*A 16th-century engraving showing the interior of a goldsmith's workshop.*

guildsman to learn a specific trade. Children began their training sometime between the ages of seven and 13. At the beginning they only did small, easy tasks in the workshop of a master, such as cleaning, running errands, and carrying materials. A master provided food, clothes, and lodging for his apprentices in exchange for their work. They received little or no wages. For between six and 10 years the master taught his apprentices his trade or craft and gradually gave them greater responsibility in the workshop.

After a boy had completed his apprenticeship, he would then be able to became a journeyman, or day laborer, in the guild. A journeyman and guild member could earn wages and look for work individually or as a member of a larger workshop. Usually, a journeyman gained experience by moving around to wherever work was available until he had saved enough money to establish a workshop of his own.

### BECOMING A MASTER

Later in their careers journeymen might try to become masters. To do so, a craftsman submitted an example of his work—a "masterpiece"—to the masters of his guild. For example, a goldsmith might make a particularly fine piece of jewelry, or a mason might submit his work on a city project such as a cathedral or guildhall. If the master guildsmen considered a journeyman's work to be of outstanding quality, the other masters would agree to grant him master status. In some cases journeymen worked for years on a single piece that they hoped would gain them the status of master guildsman.

Only master guildsmen were allowed to take on apprentices, vote in guild meetings, or serve as shareholders in the guild's business ventures. Masters also acted as judges in guild disputes; in many towns being a master guildsman was a way to gain power in government.

### WOMEN IN GUILDS

Women were rarely given the opportunity to become guild members, although a few exceptions were made in textile production, particularly in France and the Netherlands. Women often worked alongside their husbands, especially in trades such as weaving or glovemaking, but were not given the

*A 17th-century watercolor showing master guildsmen receiving a newly elected master into their guild.*

*This 17th-century woodcut shows a pair of tailors at work. Tailors' guilds were among the wealthiest institutions in Europe in the 16th and 17th centuries.*

## CHARITY AND DEFENSE

Many merchant and craft guilds took an active part in the religious life of the city by sponsoring feast days, pageants, or processions. Some guilds were originally formed more as a religious fraternity than as a craft organization. Guilds often sponsored charitable institutions as well. Guilds might collect money to build or supply hospitals and orphanages, and they frequently put on religious plays depicting the Crucifixion at Easter or the story of Christ's birth at Christmas. In the Netherlands guilds even helped form military brotherhoods or militias to defend cities in times of crisis. Guilds often provided a welfare safety net to their members when a government was not able to do so. As Europe became divided by religious changes during the Reformation, guilds became less prominent in countries that shifted toward Protestantism. However, all guilds, whether in Catholic or Protestant countries, continued to support charities and to provide much needed services to their members.

same status as the men who had been apprenticed and had worked their way through the guild system. Even if a woman was represented by the guild, she could not obtain master status or participate in guild government.

**THE DECLINE OF CRAFT GUILDS**
Merchant guilds, along with those that represented professions such as judges or notaries, were usually more powerful than craft guilds. Like craft guilds, they offered apprenticeships, regulated wages, and negotiated terms of work. Unlike the craft guilds, their members often had more money and therefore more influence in city politics. At times the merchant and craft guilds clashed over issues such as taxes on importing raw materials and quality

control on goods purchased from craftsmen for export.

Between 1500 and 1700 guilds continued as they had for centuries. However, in many parts of Europe the guilds' importance diminished, in part because of economic circumstances. For example, Italian textile production peaked around 1600. After this date the European economy slowed, disease and wars, such as the Thirty Years' War (1618–1648), reduced domestic consumption of goods and limited possibilities for export. Taxes to fund the wars hurt the purchasing power of commoners and elites alike. In addition, the French, Dutch, and English began to produce inexpensive textiles that forced higher-priced Italian goods out of the market. In such a situation guild membership was not able to protect workers from economic hardship. As textile work slowed, guild membership dropped.

## THE PUTTING-OUT SYSTEM

Another reason for the decline of the guilds lay in the development of the putting-out system. City governments did not always protect guilds and their members in crisis. When demand for a particular product fell, guilds often resisted lowering prices or cutting production. This encouraged some tradesmen to find a way around the guild system in order to find cheaper trade goods. City governments did not prevent enterprising individuals from finding country people willing to work for far less money than their urban counterparts. An entrepreneur would buy wool, for example, and have it put out to be spun in the country. The yarn could then be collected and put out to someone else for weaving; finally the cloth could be put out to yet another source for finishing. All these tasks could be carried out by laborers in the countryside who had no connection to the city guilds and who worked for lower wages than guild laborers. When the entrepreneur collected the final product and sold it to merchants, he could charge less than the guilds demanded for similar goods.

## GUILDS AND CAPITALISM

When production moved away from the city and became financed by wealthy entrepreneurs, the control of the guilds was undermined, and they became less powerful. Capitalism began to replace traditional modes of production, and guilds became less important by the late 18th century.

*A modern view of a guildhall in Antwerp, Belgium. Guilds often built large headquarters to demonstrate their wealth and power.*

SEE ALSO

- Capitalism
- Government, systems of
- Manufacturing
- Towns
- Urbanization

# GUSTAVUS ADOLPHUS

Gustav II Adolf, better known by the Latinized form of his name, Gustavus Adolphus, has been described as the greatest Swedish king and one of the great statesmen in European history. To the Protestants of Sweden and Germany he was the "Lion of the North."

Gustavus was born on December 9, 1594, the eldest son of Charles IX of Sweden and Christina of Holstein. When Gustavus ascended the throne in 1611, aged 17, he headed a nation racked by internal disputes and impoverished by simultaneous wars with Poland, Russia, and Denmark. In addition, the Riksdag (Assembly) insisted on constitutional concessions before Gustavus could take control of the government.

Skilled in the arts of diplomacy and war, Gustavus was well equipped to deal with such problems. He gave Sweden the most advanced army of its time by, for example, solving the problem of integrating infantry with cavalry actions, and deploying artillery that could move around the battlefield.

### PEACE AND WAR

In 1613 Gustavus recognized that the war with Denmark was lost and negotiated peace. He met with more success against Russia, from which he acquired territory around the Baltic Sea in 1617. The war with Poland ended in 1629, leaving Sweden the most powerful state in the Baltic region.

With the help of Chancellor Axel Oxenstierna, Gustavus united Sweden. Together they created four Estates in

*Gustavus Adolphus turned Sweden into the leading power in the Baltic region after modernizing the army. He also introduced major reforms of the government and created a secondary education system.*

the Riksdag, giving the nobles, clergy, burghers or middle class, and peasants a voice in government.

As a fierce opponent of Catholicism, in 1630 Gustavus took Sweden into the Thirty Years' War on the side of the German Protestants. However, he accepted French Catholic money to assist him in his other aim of curtailing Austrian Hapsburg power. Gustavus won many victories for the Protestants before he was killed at the Battle of Lützen on November 16, 1632.

SEE ALSO

- Christina of Sweden
- Poland-Lithuania
- Russia
- Scandinavia
- Thirty Years' War
- Northern Wars

# HAPSBURG FAMILY

In the 16th century the Hapsburgs came to rule huge areas of Europe, from Germany through the Netherlands to Spain. In doing so, they had to face the same forces that were destabilizing all of Europe, including the spread of Protestantism and the rise of competing nation-states.

The Hapsburgs originated in Switzerland, where they took their name from a castle named Habichtsburg ("Hawk's Castle"), built in 1020 by two members of the family. Over the next centuries the family acquired lands in Germany and Austria, spreading out from their main base along the Danube River. In 1273 Rudolph of Hapsburg became the king of the Germans and assumed the title Holy Roman emperor, a title that in practice meant very little outside Germany. From the 14th century the imperial crown was not passed from father to son but to a man chosen by a number of rulers and archbishops, known as the electors. However, as the Hapsburgs continued to extend their territory and power, they were able to impose their candidates on the electors. From 1438 until the empire's end in 1806 the title was virtually hereditary within the Hapsburg family.

## LOSS AND GROWTH

Despite holding the title of Holy Roman emperor, at the end of the 15th century the Hapsburgs were just one of a number of dynasties—including the Valois of France and the Jagiellons of Poland, Bohemia, and Hungary—that were in the process of expanding their territory and power. By the 1520s, however, the Hapsburgs had created the most extensive empire in Europe since the ninth century. They had embarked on a golden age for which the catalyst was the marriage policy of the Hapsburg Emperor Maximilian I (ruled 1493–1519).

In 1477 Maximilian married Mary, the only child of the duke of Burgundy and heiress to Burgundy, the Netherlands, Luxemburg, and Franche Comté. The French gained control of Burgundy, but the remaining lands passed to the son of Maximilian and Mary, Philip the Handsome. In 1496 Maximilian arranged the marriage of Philip to Joanna, heiress to the Spanish throne, thereby acquiring Spain for the

*Maximilian I, shown here with members of his family, extended the Hapsburg Empire through marriage alliances rather than warfare.*

MAXIMILIANVS I IMP ARCHIDVX AVSTRIÆ DVX BVRGVNDIÆ

PHILIPPVS HISP. REX.I. ARCHIDVX AVSTRIÆ.

MARIA DVCISSA BVRGVNDIÆ MAX: VXOR

# KEEPING IT IN THE FAMILY

Family bonds were very important to many Hapsburg rulers. Philip II, for example, relied on family members to govern distant lands or fight wars. In 1559 he made his half-sister, Margaret of Parma, governor of the Netherlands. He later appointed his half-brother, Don John of Austria, to command the fleet that defeated the Ottoman Turks at the 1571 Battle of Lepanto. Another aspect of Hapsburg family unity, however, proved disastrous. This was intermarriage, a policy the Hapsburgs pursued to prevent rival dynasties gaining power but led to interbreeding. One result was the famous "Hapsburg lip," a prominent lower lip—and often jaw—first evident on Holy Roman Emperor Frederick III (ruled 1452–1493). Another result was mental instability, which was particularly marked in the case of Charles II of Spain (ruled 1665–1700). This instability came at a very bad time for the Spanish crown, which needed a strong monarch after years of financial decline, the loss of territories to France in 1659, and a succession of ruthless aristocrats who had dominated the Spanish court.

*Charles V, king of Spain from 1516 to 1556 and Holy Roman emperor from 1519 to 1556, had a pronounced lantern jaw.*

Hapsburgs. Maximilian also used diplomacy and marriages to gain the kingdoms of Hungary and Bohemia for his family. By 1519, when his grandson was elected emperor as Charles V, the Hapsburgs ruled over enormous parts of western and eastern Europe; through Spain they also ruled lands in the Caribbean and Americas.

## LONG-TERM THREATS

Charles V set out to unify his possessions. He was hampered in doing so by three major threats to Hapsburg power. The first was the spread of the Protestant Reformation, in response to which the Hapsburgs remained strongly Catholic. Charles, for example, condemned the ideas of the religious reformer Martin Luther at the Diet (assembly) of Worms, in Germany, in 1521. The Reformation cost the Hapsburgs dearly. Hapsburg leaders regarded it as their duty to repel the advances of Protestantism wherever they could. In turn, however, religious dissidents challenged their rule across their territories. In Germany enormous religious and social divisions led to the Peasants' Revolt of 1525, the largest popular uprising in European history. The uprising was suppressed, with about 100,000 peasants being killed in the fighting.

The second threat to Hapsburg power was rivalry with France. Between 1519 and 1558 much of this rivalry centered on Italy, as both Charles and Francis I of France attempted to outdo each other in the influence they could exert over Italian city-states, as well as the papacy in Rome.

The third threat was posed by the Ottoman Turks who had captured Constantinople (present-day Istanbul) in 1453 and for centuries had been making inroads into Europe. For Charles V the Muslim Turks were a threat not only to his lands but also to his concept of a Christian Europe. He and his successors waged expensive campaigns against the Turks, who defeated the Hungarian army in 1526 before advancing into Austria and briefly besieging Vienna in 1529.

The threats were interrelated. The French were prepared to support Protestants and even Turks if they considered it would damage their Hapsburg enemies. Furthermore, the threats remained with the Hapsburgs for the rest of the 1500s and well into the 1600s. Charles V, realizing that the Hapsburg Empire had become too big for any one ruler, split it in two. He left the German lands—and the opportunity to be elected Holy Roman emperor—to his brother, Ferdinand. The rest—Spain, the Netherlands, and possessions in Italy—passed to his son, Philip II (ruled 1556–1598), on Charles's abdication.

## RELIGION AND WAR

A fervent champion of Catholicism, Philip II was determined to crush the Calvinist form of Protestantism that had spread throughout Dutch society. However, his policies, including a "reign of terror" against Calvinists led by his lieutenant, the duke of Alva, only succeeded in fueling opposition to Hapsburg rule. Philip spent vast sums of money in an attempt that ultimately failed. In 1648 his grandson, Philip IV, formally acknowledged the existence of an independent Protestant Dutch republic, the United Provinces, while retaining control over the southern Netherlands (modern-day Belgium).

Religious differences and rivalry with France—as well as other nations—also brought trouble for the Hapsburgs. In the 1620s Holy Roman Emperor Ferdinand II (ruled 1619–1637) introduced a number of

FERDINANDVS. ARCH:AVST:

strict pro-Catholic measures, including the expulsion of Protestants first from Bohemia and then from his German lands. Ferdinand's armies initially had great success. But his policies angered many rulers, including some German electors. The kings of France and Sweden intervened.

This series of conflicts was known as the Thirty Years' War (1618–1648). By the late 1640s Hapsburg losses were so great that Ferdinand III, Ferdinand II's son, had no choice but to sign the Peace of Westphalia (1648), which granted territories to France and Sweden, permitted freedom of belief within the Holy Roman Empire—apart from the Hapsburgs' hereditary lands— and granted rulers of individual German states greater independence. The golden age of the Hapsburgs had ended.

*This is a portrait of Ferdinand I (ruled 1558 –1564). On the death of his older brother, Holy Roman Emperor Charles V, in 1558 Ferdinand became emperor.*

### SEE ALSO

- Charles V
- Holy Roman Empire
- Lepanto, Battle of
- Netherlands, Revolt of the
- Ottoman Empire
- Philip II
- Spain
- Thirty Years' War

# HENRY OF NAVARRE

Henry of Navarre (1553–1610) became the first Bourbon king of France as Henry IV. He led the French Protestants during the Wars of Religion (1562–1598). He converted to Catholicism to secure his throne and managed to bring religious stability to France.

*Henry of Navarre, shown in this 16th-century portrait, became king as Henry IV in 1589. Although he was raised as a Protestant, he converted to Catholicism in 1593 to secure his throne and resolve the religious disputes that blighted France.*

**B**orn in Pau, France, on December 13, 1553, Henry was the son of Antoine de Bourbon, king of Navarre, and Jeanne d'Albret. Henry's mother raised him as a Protestant.

### RELIGIOUS DIFFERENCES
In 1572 Henry married Margaret of Valois. The union was arranged by her mother, the Catholic regent of France, Catherine de Médicis, in an effort to resolve the Wars of Religion. Within a week, however, the Saint Bartholomew's Day Massacre occurred in which thousands of Huguenots, or French Protestants, were murdered by Catholic forces. Henry led a Huguenot force that resisted the attacks but was captured and held prisoner for several years. He escaped in 1576 and agreed to a favorable peace for the Huguenots.

In 1589 King Henry III died, leaving Henry of Navarre next in line to the throne. However, the Catholic League, a national organization of Catholics, refused to recognize him as their king. Henry defeated the league's army at Ivry in 1590, but Paris remained its stronghold. Henry could not break the city's defenses, so in 1593 he resorted to diplomacy. Recognizing that French Catholics would never accept a Protestant king, he converted to Catholicism, famously saying, "Paris is worth a Mass." He was finally crowned in 1594.

In the Edict of Nantes of 1598 Henry recognized religious toleration for Huguenots. Despite Henry's work to resolve ongoing religious problems in France, he was treated with suspicion by Catholics. In 1610 Henry was killed in Paris by a fanatical Catholic.

SEE ALSO
• Catherine de Médicis
• France
• French Wars of Religion
• Huguenots

# HERESY AND HERETICS

In the 13th century the Christian church became more determined than ever to act against individuals and groups who in any way questioned its declared doctrines. Persecution of these dissenters—called heretics— reached a peak in the 16th century as a result of the Reformation.

The church had fought to stamp out teachings that went against the beliefs of the majority since the second century. In 325 A.D. a council summoned by the Roman Emperor Constantine produced a creed, or set of statements, that laid down the core beliefs of Christianity. Any deviation from such beliefs was heresy, a word that comes from the Greek word for "choice."

Heretics chose to follow their own beliefs rather than those sanctioned by the church. For centuries heresy was

*Katherine Cawches and her two daughters are burned for heresy on the island of Guernsey in July 1556.*

more often found in individuals than in groups. However, from the 12th century several movements challenged the church's authority, causing it to search for a better way to fight heresy.

## THE INQUISITION

In 1231 Pope Gregory IX (pope 1227–1241) set up a procedure known as the Inquisition to seek out and interrogate suspected heretics and punish those found guilty. Offenders might be flogged, fined, or made to go on a pilgrimage. More serious was excommunication—being excluded from the company of fellow Christians and from receiving the holy sacraments. The ultimate punishment for heretics was being burned at the stake.

In the late 15th century the Spanish monarchs tried to enforce Catholicism in a drive to unify the country. They used the Spanish Inquisition to help them achieve this. Originally set up to purify the country of heresy, it became a useful political tool. The tribunals often focused on Muslims and Jews who had converted to Catholicism, but who were suspected of secretly keeping their old faiths. The church struggled to curb the Inquisition's excesses, which terrified the local population.

The church also assessed the work of intellectuals and scientists for signs of heresy. It saw itself as the guardian and sole interpreter of the scriptures. For example, the Inquisition in Italy tried Galileo, a scientist who supported Copernicus's theory that the earth moved around the sun. He was sentenced to house arrest for life.

## THE REFORMATION

During the Reformation the Catholic church used charges of heresy to try to stamp out Protestant ideas. German reformer Martin Luther was charged with heresy in 1520. His works were

burned; and when he refused to retract his beliefs, he was excommunicated.

The Protestant reformers believed that the Bible, rather than the church, was the supreme authority. The mainstream reformers encouraged people to read the Bible for themselves; but unlike the radical sects, such as the Anabaptists, they did not believe that individuals were free to interpret the Bible as they wished.

Protestant reformers often engaged in fierce debate among themselves on doctrinal matters. They regarded heresy just as seriously as the Catholic church

*The Spaniard Michael Servetus is burned as a heretic in Geneva on October 27, 1553. He was regarded as a heretic both by Protestants and Catholics.*

and were often equally intolerant of differing views. However, they were usually in a minority and lacked the backing of secular rulers to prosecute heretics. Their main concern was to spread their ideas and avoid persecution.

In the Protestant stronghold of Geneva, however, John Calvin tried the Spanish theologian Michael Servetus for heresy in 1553. Servetus rejected the Christian idea of the Trinity—that there is one God who exists in three persons: the Father, the Son, and the Holy Spirit. He had already been condemned by the Inquisition. The Genevans found him guilty, and he was burned at the stake.

### RELIGIOUS TOLERANCE

Servetus's death inspired the Protestant thinker Sebastian Castellio (1515–1563) to publish a book pleading for greater tolerance. Declaring that a heretic is simply "a man with whom you disagree," he tried to show how dangerous it was to assume that truth was rigid and should be defended by the taking of life.

Castellio was one of the first to call for a more tolerant view of religious disagreements. During the 17th

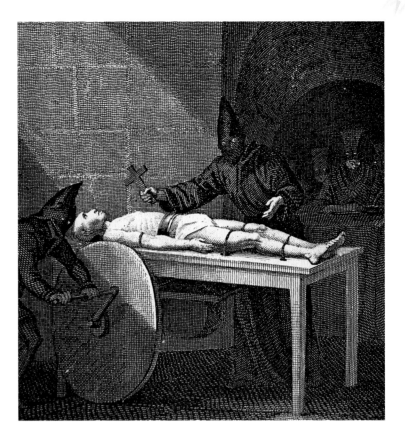

century executing people on religious grounds became increasingly rare as religious divisions became permanent, and the idea of toleration was gradually accepted. During the Reformation period, however, historians estimated that perhaps as many as 5,000 people were executed for their religious beliefs.

*A suspected Spanish heretic is tortured. The Inquisition in Spain was particularly ruthless in its use of torture following the appointment in 1483 of Tomás de Torquemada as Grand Inquisitor.*

## HERETICAL TEXTS

One of the ways in which the Catholic church attempted to prevent heretical teachings from spreading was by banning theological, scientific, and other types of book that it believed would corrupt people. A list of forbidden books, officially known as the *Index Librorum Prohibitorum*, was issued by Pope Paul IV in 1557. A few years later Pope Pius V set up a special committee charged with updating the list. Once the list had been drawn up, it would be passed to inquisitors in Catholic countries, who would then visit local printers and booksellers and warn them, on threat of excommunication, not to produce or handle the banned books. Many distinguished authors and works suffered as a result of the *Index*. Scientific works by Copernicus and Galileo were prohibited, as were books by later authors such as the 18th-century English historian Edward Gibbon and the 19th-century German philosopher Immanuel Kant. The *Index* was abolished only in 1966.

**SEE ALSO**

- Catholic church
- Inquisition
- Reformation
- Religious dissent

# HIDEYOSHI TOYOTOMI

Toyotomi Hideyoshi (1537–1598) completed the work of the Japanese warlord Oda Nobunaga in unifying his country, ending two centuries of war between rival clans and preparing the way for Tokugawa Ieyasu to become shogun, or military dictator.

Hideyoshi was born in Owari Province, Japan, in 1537. His father was a peasant who had served in the army of the leading Oda clan. As a boy Hideyoshi worked in a temple and later entered the service of the Daimyo (feudal warlord) Imagawa Yoshimoto. In 1557 Hideyoshi went to work under General Oda Nobunaga. Nobunaga entrusted Hideyoshi with secret missions to win over the armies of enemy daimyos. Hideyoshi rose quickly through the ranks from samurai to general. Such advancement was unheard of in 16th-century Japan, with its rigid class system.

## MILITARY SUCCESSES

Hideyoshi helped Nobunaga unify Japan by suppressing warring clans in the country. He later became a revered military leader himself. In 1582 Oda Nobunaga was assasinated, and Hideyoshi avenged his death by crushing the leader of the clan responsible, Akechi Mitushide. The emperor of Japan made Hideyoshi regent for settling clan disputes and also bestowed on him the family name of Toyotomi, following the Japanese tradition of name-giving based on great achievements. Japan was finally unified only in 1591.

*This contemporary print shows the 16th-century Japanese regent Toyotomi Hideyoshi and his horse, both ready for battle.*

As regent, Hideyoshi separated the social classes of Japan, introducing such policies as his Edict on Changing Status, which forbade villagers from moving to towns, and the Sword Hunt, which prevented peasants from receiving military training.

This strict organization of Japanese society lasted for over 250 years. After Hideyoshi's death rule of Japan fell to the warlord Tokugawa Ieyasu.

SEE ALSO

- Japan
- Warfare

# HOBBES, THOMAS

Thomas Hobbes (1588–1679) was an English philosopher who pioneered modern political science. His main contribution was his argument for the state's claim to absolute authority over its subjects in his political treatise *Leviathan*, published in 1651.

Born in the south of England, on April 5, 1588, Hobbes was educated at Oxford University. In 1603 he entered the service of the Cavendish family, the earls of Devonshire, as a tutor. His association with the Cavendish family provided him with access to an extensive library and helped him make connections with leading intellectuals.

Hobbes traveled widely in Europe. He met the French philosopher René Descartes (1596–1650) and the Italian physicist and astronomer Galileo Galilei (1564–1642). In 1646 he became tutor to the prince of Wales, the future King Charles II, while the English court was in exile in Paris during the English Civil War.

## THE WORKS OF HOBBES

Hobbes's *Leviathan, or the Matter, Form, and Power of a Commonwealth, Ecclesiastical and Civil* (1651) is viewed as a masterpiece of political philosophy. In it Hobbes argued that in a presocial state men were in continual conflict with one another. Human life was "nasty, brutish, and short." For self-preservation rational men formed a commonwealth that placed all power in the hands of a sovereign authority, preferably a single ruler. They accepted a form of social contract under which they agreed to surrender certain rights in return for protection from the state. Reason, not God's will, was the basis of political life. During his life Hobbes was accused of being an atheist by clergymen because his work challenged God's role as supreme creator.

Hobbes wrote other works on government, including *The Elements of Law* (published 1650), in which he defended absolute sovereignty of the king, and *On the State* (1642).

After the monarchy was restored in England in 1660, Hobbes's former pupil, Charles II, gave him a pension. Hobbes died in England in 1679.

*Thomas Hobbes continued to write and publish his political and scientific ideas until he was in his 90th year.*

SEE ALSO

- Descartes, René
- English Civil War
- Government, systems of
- Locke, John
- Monarchy and absolutism
- Philosophy

# HOLY ROMAN EMPIRE

**Centered on Germany, the Holy Roman Empire was intended to unite the whole of western Christendom under one sovereign who ruled with the approval of the pope. In practice, the emperor and pope were often in conflict, and few monarchs felt bound to acknowledge the emperor.**

The Frankish king Charlemagne revived the concept of the Roman Empire when he had himself crowned emperor in Rome on Christmas Day 800 A.D. However, the Holy Roman Empire is usually said to date from 962, when Pope John XII crowned Otto I, king of the Germans, as Roman emperor. The word "holy" was added to the title two centuries later, during the reign of Frederick I.

In 1356 the empire gained a written constitution when Emperor Charles IV issued the Golden Bull. This document attempted to fix the rights of the leaders of the German states.

The bull established the right of seven electors to vote for a new emperor. (The number rose to nine in the 17th century.) Only certain German princes and archbishops could become electors (*see box p. 45*). The bull

*Charles V and Pope Clement VII enter Bologna for the emperor's coronation in February 1530. Charles had been elected emperor many years before, in 1519.*

also established an assembly, or Diet, consisting of three Estates: the electors, other members of the nobility, and representatives of the imperial cities. The Estates met separately, and the approval of all three, plus that of the emperor, was required to resolve any matter put before them.

## EMPIRE IN DECLINE

In the empire there were two kingships: a primary northern kingship in Germany and a secondary southern kingship in Lombardy in Italy. In practice the emperor had no political power in Italy. His position was stronger in Germany, but even there his power was limited. Germany was made up of numerous independent states and "free towns," none of which wished to be ruled by the emperor.

By 1500 the power of the emperor was waning. This was partly because the electors generally chose candidates who would not interfere with their privileges. There was no centralized government, while the Diet met infrequently and found it difficult to exercise authority. The ties with Rome were loosening. Frederick III (ruled 1452–1493) was the last emperor to be crowned in Rome; his great-grandson Charles V (ruled 1519–1556) was the last emperor crowned by the pope. Both Frederick III and Charles V were members of the Hapsburg Dynasty, from which the electors had selected all the emperors since 1438.

## CHARLES V

A large area of Europe was united under Hapsburg rule during the reign of Charles V, who was king of Spain from 1516. This meant that his election as Holy Roman emperor in 1519 offered real possibilities for reform. In particular, he had the power to invest authority in the Imperial Council, or

Reichregiment, so that it could implement the laws passed by the Diet. Charles V had a powerful and influential ally in Frederick III, elector

*This map shows the extent of the Holy Roman Empire in 1600.*

# THE ELECTORS

Those princes whose claim to the title of Elector of the Empire was recognized in the Golden Bull of 1356 were the real holders of power within the Holy Roman Empire because they elected each new Holy Roman emperor. They were the prince archbishops of Cologne, Trier, and Mainz, the king of Bohemia, the duke of Saxony, the count Palatine of the Rhine, and the marquess of Brandenburg. Their number and titles remained unchanged until after the Thirty Years' War in 1648, when the Duchy of Bavaria, ruled by the Wittelsbachs, was elevated to the Electorate. This gave the Wittelsbach family two votes since they also held the Palatinate of the Rhine.

In 1692 the duke of Brunswick-Luneburg-Hannover became elector of Hannover. Just before the collapse of the empire, Emperor Napoleon of France imposed his own reorganization, creating three lay electors (Hesse-Cassel, Baden, and Württemberg) and one ecclesiastical elector, the archbishop of Salzburg, while the archbishops of Mainz, Trier, and Cologne lost their electoral rank. This outside interference in the affairs of the empire made its weakness and vulnerability evident and was one of the reasons why it was finally dissolved.

of Saxony and president of the Reichregiment, who had been instrumental in securing the election of Charles. However, the events of the Reformation then put these two men on opposing sides. Frederick provided protection to Martin Luther and Luther's fellow reformer, Philip Melanchthon, and in 1520 he refused to implement the papal bull excommunicating Luther. Meanwhile Charles, an ardent Catholic, was forced to watch from the sidelines as Germany split into warring states.

## A DIVIDED EMPIRE

Many German princes and nobles adopted the Lutheran doctrine for reasons other than religion. Although they were content to see the Hapsburgs lead European resistance against the Ottoman Turks, many German princes and nobles were alarmed by the growth of the Hapsburg Empire under Charles V. Conversion to Protestantism gave them a legitimate means of challenging Charles's power as Holy Roman emperor while seizing the wealth and property of the church. Since the subjects of a converting ruler had to convert also, tithes that had been due to the church were now paid to the ruler.

On Luther's death in 1546 his doctrines were condemned by the Council of Trent and his followers defeated in the Schmalkaldic War. However, in 1555 the Peace of Augsburg recognized the legal existence of Lutheranism, though not that of Calvinism. This was to be a cause of continuing tensions within the empire following the abdication of Charles in

1556 and the election of his brother Ferdinand I as emperor. The grandson of Ferdinand I, Ferdinand III, became Holy Roman emperor in 1619. A staunch supporter of the Counter Reformation, he provoked a Protestant revolt in Bohemia, of which he was king. The revolt led to the Thirty Years' War (1618–1648).

Following the Peace of Westphalia in 1648, the Holy Roman Empire was little more than a loose confederation of more than 350 virtually independent states. The emperor was merely nominal head of the central European Catholics. Occasionally, sufficient imperial cooperation could be stimulated to meet external threats, such as the westward expansion of the Ottoman Empire or Louis XIV's efforts to expand France eastward into German territory.

The empire lingered on until 1806, when it was absorbed into the empire ruled by Napoleon. It was not revived following Napoleon's downfall in 1815.

*The crown of the Holy Roman emperor was placed on his head during his coronation. For centuries the coronation was conducted by the pope in Italy, but from 1530 it took place in Germany without the pope's involvement.*

SEE ALSO

- Austria
- Bohemia
- Counter Reformation
- Germany
- Hapsburg family
- Papacy
- Reformation
- Thirty Years' War

# HOUSES AND FURNITURE

**Houses, and the way in which they were furnished, varied enormously in the period between 1500 and 1700. While the homes of the poor were extremely basic and changed little from medieval times, the houses of wealthier members of society grew to have more rooms and furniture.**

The differing climates across Europe affected the design of houses in different regions. In hot countries such as Italy and Spain, for example, buildings had small windows and thick walls to keep out the heat of the sun. In countries with heavy snowfall, such as Switzerland and Germany, houses were designed with steeply sloping roofs so that the snow would fall off and not build up.

### BUILDING MATERIALS

The type of building materials available locally also influenced the way houses were built. Good quality stone was a hard-wearing and desirable material, and was widely used throughout Europe. However, it could not always be quarried locally and was expensive to transport because of its weight. In regions with abundant woods and forests, such as England, houses were often built with frames made from timber. In areas with good supplies of natural clays, such as Holland and Belgium, bricks were widely used. Roofing materials included stone, slate, clay tiles, and thatching made from reeds or straw.

The vast majority of the population lived in the countryside during the 16th and 17th centuries. Historians

estimate that in 1600 around 75 percent of people in western and central Europe were rural dwellers. Many were peasants and landless laborers who lived in extremely primitive conditions. Typically their

*These timber-framed houses in the French town of Troyes date from the 16th century.*

homes consisted of just one room, where the family cooked, ate, and slept. Often farm animals were kept in an adjoining room. Floors were commonly made from beaten earth and were strewn with reeds or straw. Poor families owned very little furniture, and what they did have was extremely basic; it might include a few wooden shelves, stools, chests, and a table.

More prosperous members of the rural community, such as farmers and millers, lived in more comfort. They had larger homes with more rooms. In England, for example, farmhouses evolved from medieval times, when they had been centered around a large, open communal room—a design known as a hall house. By 1600 new farmhouses were being built with two separate rooms—a parlor and a kitchen—on the ground floor and two bedrooms upstairs. The rooms were heated by fireplaces in a central chimney, which was itself a new development. Some larger houses had glazed windows, but many were unglazed because glass remained an expensive luxury. Floors were surfaced with flagstones, clay tiles, or wooden floorboards. Furniture was still simple but might include a selection of chairs, benches, stools, tables, cupboards, sideboards, dressers, chests, and beds.

### COUNTRY HOUSES

The changing design of houses to include more rooms with specific functions—such as bedrooms for sleeping, a parlor for relaxing and entertaining—reflected people's desire for privacy. These changes were most obvious in the large houses of the land-owning gentry and nobles, such as the châteaus built by French courtiers in the Loire River valley.

# BEDS AND BED CHAMBERS

Beds were often the most valuable pieces of furniture people owned in the 16th and 17th centuries. They ranged from simple box beds to luxurious four-poster beds, with decorated headboards and posts supporting a tester, or canopy, from which hung curtains of fabrics.

Most extravagant of all were the state bedchambers in 17th-century royal palaces. These large, ornately furnished rooms were extremely expensive status symbols. Members of the royal family or their distinguished guests went to these chambers accompanied by many attendants and followers. After he or she had been disrobed and put to bed, and the courtiers had left, the sleeper would retire to a smaller and more comfortable bedroom situated behind the state apartment.

*This bedroom in Boscobel House, England, is furnished as it would have been in the 17th century. The house was once a prosperous farm.*

Large houses were still centered around a grand hall. However, while in medieval times this space had served as a dining room and sleeping quarters for the whole household, during the 16th century it came to be used solely for entertaining. The lord of the house had always had a few private rooms at one end of the hall, and in the 16th century these increased in number to include withdrawing rooms (later known as drawing rooms), dining rooms, studies, bedchambers, and garde robes (primitive toilets). These rooms were located in wings of buildings sited at either end of the hall or around a courtyard. A separate wing housed service facilities, such as kitchens, pantries, and laundries.

## PALACES

In palaces the number of state rooms used for entertaining grew. Whole suites of lavishly decorated and furnished chambers were designed to receive guests and visiting dignitaries. Furniture was usually arranged around the edges of the rooms and was set out as required for functions. It included stools, chairs, thrones, tables, cabinets, mirrors, and candle stands made from elaborately carved or sculpted wood. Sometimes furniture was inlaid with patterns in different colored woods, stones, or precious metals, or in some cases it was entirely covered with silver. King Louis XIV's remodeling of the royal palace at Versailles (1661–1710) is the largest and most opulent example of 17th-century palace design.

## TOWN HOUSES

In towns and cities the shape of houses was influenced by the limited amount of land available. Houses were usually taller and narrower than those in the countryside, and were often part of a continuous row or terrace. The pressure

on land was nowhere more pronounced than in Amsterdam, which in the 17th century grew immensely prosperous from its trade with the East Indies. Dutch merchants built terraces of tall, narrow houses on sites hemmed in by canals. These buildings were often six or seven stories high and had only a few rooms per floor. They had very steep, narrow staircases, to save space, and large windows. Furniture had to be hoisted into upstairs rooms through the windows using a pulley mounted at the top of the building. The furnishings reflected their owners' wealth and the countries with which the city traded. Chairs, tables, and cabinets in these Dutch homes often incorporated exotic materials and techniques from Asia, such as tortoiseshell and lacquer work.

*The back of this 17th-century Spanish armchair is decorated with carved heraldic motifs. The seat would originally have had a cushion.*

SEE ALSO
• Architecture
• Decorative arts
• Families
• Privacy and luxury
• Textiles
• Versailles

# HUDSON, HENRY

**Henry Hudson was a 17th-century English navigator who undertook four voyages in search of quick sea passages to East Asia. His name was given to the Hudson River and Hudson Bay, which he was credited with discovering in 1609 and 1610 respectively.**

No one knows when Henry Hudson was born, and there are no details of his life until 1607, when he was hired by the English Muscovy Company to navigate the northeast passage, a hoped-for sea route between the Atlantic and Pacific oceans along the Arctic coast of Eurasia. The aim of the voyage was to find a way to China, Japan, and the East Indies that was faster than the established route around the Cape of Good Hope, at the southern tip of Africa. Hudson set off in a small vessel with 11 sailors, but his progress was blocked by pack ice.

### FURTHER VOYAGES

In 1608 Hudson embarked on his second voyage and reached Novaya Zemlya, a Russian island in the Arctic Ocean, before he was halted again by ice. In 1609 Hudson undertook a third voyage with his son, this time for the Dutch East India Company. While in Amsterdam Hudson heard about the existence of a northwest passage between the Atlantic and the Pacific to the north of North America but agreed with his employers to return if he could not find a northeast passage. When his ship, the *Half Moon*, was slowed by storms, Hudson ignored his orders and sailed west. Reaching North America, he explored up the Hudson River—now named for him—to Albany, giving the Dutch their claim to New York.

On his way back to the Netherlands Hudson stopped off in England, where he was arrested for helping an enemy power. By 1610, however, Hudson was freed, and he set off again in search of the northwest passage. He sailed his new ship, *Discovery*, up the Davis Strait between Greenland and Baffin Island, into Hudson Bay—also now named for him. Failing to find an outlet to the Pacific, he spent the winter in the bay, suffering great hardship.

### A MYSTERIOUS DEATH

Food was scarce, and the crew became increasingly disillusioned. In spring 1611 they mutinied and cast their captain, his son, and eight sick sailors adrift in Hudson Bay in a small open boat with few provisions. Hudson is believed to have died soon afterward.

*This engraving made in 1856 shows Henry Hudson meeting local peoples on the bank of the Hudson River in around 1600.*

SEE ALSO
- Canada
- Exploration
- New York
- North America
- Ships

# HUGUENOTS

During the 16th and 17th centuries French Protestants were called Huguenots. They followed the reformed faith of John Calvin and were well organized religiously and politically. For most of the period they were subject to harsh persecution and repression.

After the Reformation began in Germany in 1517, growing numbers of people in other countries, including France, were attracted to the reformers' ideas. They became known as Protestants. There was little toleration of religious difference in Catholic France, and Protestants were persecuted from the outset. In 1536 a royal edict condemned them as heretics and urged their extermination. Some Protestants fled to lands where they could live in safety.

### CALVINIST FOUNDATIONS
One early refugee, the reformer John Calvin (1509–1564), was to be very influential in the development of Protestantism in France. He wrote a clear statement of Protestant beliefs in his *Institutes of the Christian Religion* (1536) and later organized the city-state of Geneva in Switzerland as a Christian state. Both of these achievements served as models for Protestants elsewhere. Calvin also trained church ministers, many of whom were French nobles, and then supported them when they returned to their home countries.

By the 1550s most French reformers were Calvinists. The founding of the Huguenot church in Paris in 1555 and its first synod (meeting of church leaders) in 1559 marked the beginning of a rapid increase in French Calvinism. While 15 churches were represented at

the 1559 synod, 2,150 were represented at a synod held in 1661. By the 1560s around 10 percent of the French population—some 1.8 million people—was Protestant. The main Huguenot areas were in the south, from Gascony in the west to Dauphiné in the east.

Many Huguenots were aristocrats or skilled craftworkers. Historians speculate that they were drawn to the new religion for a number of reasons. They were the most literate members of society, with ready access to new ideas, and were attracted by Calvin's emphasis on individual faith and individual interpretation of the Bible. The Calvinist emphasis on self-reliance was also in line with the ethos of hardworking craftsmen. It offered a strong alternative to the weakness and continued corruption of the French

*This stone Huguenot house, built between 1692 and 1712, stands in New Palz, in New York state. New Palz was established by Huguenots who fled from France in 1685 when King Louis XIV ended their freedom to worship as they chose.*

Catholic church. In the case of the nobility the Huguenot faith also became tied up with the broader power struggles of influential families and factions at the royal court.

## WARS OF RELIGION

The Huguenot aim to secure freedom of worship and equality with other French subjects became intertwined with bitter court rivalries and a struggle to gain the French throne in the so-called Wars of Religion. From 1562 France was wracked by bloody and disjointed civil wars for some 40 years. One of the nastiest actions occurred in 1572, when, with the connivance of the crown, thousands of Huguenots were killed in the Saint Bartholomew's Day Massacre. As war followed war, both Protestant and Catholic towns became virtual republics. Royal authority was lost to powerful local nobles. In the south Huguenots formed the United Provinces of the Midi, a Protestant state within a state.

An end to the religious conflict and faction fighting came in 1593, when King Henry IV (ruled 1589–1610), a Huguenot, converted to Catholicism to secure his rule. In 1598 he issued the Edict of Nantes, which granted Huguenots freedom to worship and full civil rights. It also allowed them to keep their existing strongholds.

## ASSERTION OF ROYAL POWER

The edict secured an uneasy peace, but by the 1620s fighting had again broken out. The powerful chief minister Cardinal Richelieu and King Louis XIII (ruled 1610–1643) set about curbing Huguenot powers, which they saw as a direct threat to the creation of a strong monarchy. A revolt by the Huguenot stronghold of La Rochelle (1625–1628) confirmed them in their course of action. Richelieu crushed the

uprising and destroyed other Huguenot strongholds. The Treaty of Alès (1629) removed the political and military powers of the Huguenots but permitted them freedom of worship.

## REPRESSION AND EXILE

Anti-Huguenot feeling increased during the reign of Louis XIV (ruled 1643–1715), particularly as the king pursued the consolidation of his royal authority. Adhering to the rule "one king, one law, one faith," he backed the forcible conversion of Huguenots to Catholicism. In 1682 he banned Huguenots from court appointments. Then in 1685 he issued the Edict of Fontainebleau. This law revoked the toleration guaranteed by the Edict of Nantes and authorized the destruction of Huguenot churches. More than 400,000 Huguenots emigrated, many going to the Netherlands, England, Germany, and the Americas.

The Huguenots who remained were subjected to harsh repression. However, not all submitted. In the mountainous regions of Bas-Languedoc and Cévennes in southern France armed Protestants known as the Camisards mounted a rebellion in 1702 that took royal troops years to crush. Although much reduced in number, Protestants survived in France.

*Catholic soldiers attack and kill Huguenots in the massacre of Saint Bartholomew's Day in Paris on August 24, 1572. Around 3,000 Huguenots lost their lives in the French capital in the massacre; more than 20,000 were killed in the provinces.*

SEE ALSO

• Calvin, John
• France
• French Wars of Religion
• Geneva
• Henry of Navarre
• Reformation

# HUMANISM

**Underpinned by a belief in the supreme importance of human beings, Renaissance humanism encompassed a variety of literary and scholarly activities. It transformed learning and education in the 16th and 17th centuries, based on rediscovered Latin and Greek texts.**

Humanists were the intellectuals of their age, and they firmly believed in restoring the arts and texts that had passed into relative obscurity. The humanists' view of their age as a rebirth of the classical civilizations of the Greeks and Romans led historians to call this time the Renaissance, or rebirth, of learning.

While modern historians stress the continuity between the Middle Ages and the Renaissance, the latter age had many unique characteristics. Humanists viewed the ancient writers of Greece and Rome with respect because they believed that they had excelled in the study of rhetoric, poetry, history, and moral philosophy. Humanists considered these disciplines to be valuable in instructing Christians on how to achieve the ideal life.

The humanist revival entailed studying the classics, editing obscure existing classical manuscripts, and teaching the classics in universities and to the children of the nobility. Many humanists were laymen rather than clerics and were teachers or secretaries in Renaissance courts.

## ITALIAN HUMANISM

Francesco Petrarch (1304–1374) is known as the father of Italian Renaissance humanism. A poet who observed human emotions for their own sake, he also pioneered the study of classical texts. Among the many who followed in his footsteps was Niccolò Machiavelli (1469–1527), a statesman in the republic of Florence and a political theorist. He was one of a number of scholars who developed the idea of "civic humanism." In the belief that exercising social responsibility was praiseworthy, they promoted active participation in public life.

## NORTHERN HUMANISM

As a result of the invention of printing in the 15th century, humanist ideas spread from Italy to most of western Europe. Northern Renaissance humanists also cultivated knowledge of the classics. However, they are called "Christian humanists" because their scholarship focused on early Christianity. Interest in early Christian

*The Dutch humanist Erasmus gives a lecture in Brussels in 1511 to the young future Holy Roman Emperor Charles V. Erasmus spent many years traveling around Europe, giving lectures and taking part in debates with other scholars.*

writings led Christian humanists to master the ancient Greek language. The most influential of the Christian humanists was Desiderius Erasmus (1466–1536), who formulated and popularized Christian humanism while traveling extensively in Europe. By 1500 Erasmus was concentrating on reconciling the classics and Christianity. He edited the Greek text of the New Testament from the earliest available manuscript and published it in 1516. This important text provided the basis for more accurate translations of the Bible than the standard authorized Latin Vulgate Bible, which contained many errors and inconsistencies.

Erasmus's English counterpart was Thomas More (1478–1535), who also translated Greek authors and wrote in Latin. More often prayed, and many praised More's household as an ideal model of Christian family life.

### HUMANIST EDUCATION

The ideal of a humanist education, while it persisted into the 17th century, was reserved for the privileged and the male. The few women who benefited from receiving a humanist education could not pursue the professions of their male counterparts. Women were encouraged to read and study classical and Christian texts primarily to be more interesting companions for their husbands. Women who had received a humanist training would also be equipped to provide their children with an educational background that would assist them in becoming valued domestic partners.

*This portrait of Thomas More by Hans Holbein the Younger dates from 1527. A lawyer and statesman, More was also a leading humanist.*

# ERASMUS OF ROTTERDAM

The Dutch humanist scholar Desiderius Erasmus (1466–1536) contributed to Christian humanism in many ways. He produced many editions of the Bible, early Christian works, and the classics, which had a major impact on scholars throughout Europe. He hoped that educational reform would produce pious Christians who could best fulfill their social roles. During a trip to England Erasmus met the English humanist Thomas More (1478–1535) and wrote one of his most popular works, a satire entitled *The Praise of Folly* (1511). In keeping with his promotion of religious and educational reform, Erasmus used a character named Lady Folly to mock human vice and religious corruption.

**SEE ALSO**

- Bibles and bible studies
- Courts and courtiers
- Italian states
- Medici family
- Renaissance
- Schools and schooling
- Urbanization
- Women

# INCA EMPIRE

The Incas were a people who created a vast, but short-lived, empire based in the Andes Mountains on the western side of South America. The empire reached its pinnacle in the late 1400s and early 1500s but was overthrown by the Spanish in the 1530s.

In the 15th and 16th centuries what we now call the Inca Empire was known as Tahuantinsuyu, meaning "the land of the four quarters." The Incas began to conquer their neighbors around Cuzco, their highland capital city, in the late 14th century. However, it was not until around 1440 that they began a serious program of conquest. They created an empire that extended 2,600 miles (4,200km) along the coast from modern Ecuador to southern Chile, incorporating Peru, Bolivia, and parts of Argentina. The Incas built their empire on top of complex civilizations that had existed in the Andes for over 3,000 years.

Around 12 million people lived in the empire in demanding environmental conditions thanks to high altitude. They were highly organized by the government, which imposed a tax that required large numbers of people to work on building projects throughout the empire. Most people were farmers who produced their own food and clothing. Because there was no form of money in the Inca Empire, they exchanged their products or labor for whatever else they needed.

### THE SYSTEM OF AGRICULTURE
The people of the Andes developed a system of agriculture that depended on altitude. At the lowest altitudes they grew corn; slightly higher up they planted potatoes; and at the highest levels, above the tree line, they herded llamas, their most important beast of burden and source of meat. Few large

*High in the Andes Mountains stand the remains of Machu Picchu, an Inca town that was inhabited by royalty and other dignitaries during the 16th century.*

# INCA MUMMIES

Many aspects of Inca life focused on caring for and respecting the mummies of past leaders. Cuzco, a city of 100,000 residents, was also full of palaces where mummies lived. The mummies were rich and powerful, continuing to control servants, land, resources, herds of llama, textiles, and jewels. The mummies took part in public celebrations in the main square of Cuzco. Here they were carried out in procession and given food (the food was later burned) and drinks that were poured down a drain. Through this ceremony the population retained a sense of their lineage, their history, and their customs. The Catholic church continued to discover these mummies still hidden in caves in the 17th century, along with many other traditional symbols of Andean religion, including sacred stones and images.

goods were moved entirely by human porters and llamas. The Inca roads and trails were some of the greatest ever built, winding through mountains and over yawning chasms and fast-flowing rivers. The Incas also had roadside inns available for travelers. Inca buildings, or at least their foundations, survive today, consisting of immense stones fitted together tightly like pieces of a puzzle, without mortar to hold them in place.

## INCA RELIGION

The Incas worshiped a number of gods, headed by Inti, the sun god. The most important temple dedicated to Inti was the huge Corincancha in Cuzco. It had a band of solid gold running along its walls. Inti and the other gods were worshiped with offerings and animal and human sacrifices.

The Incas believed they had been chosen to rule their world and claimed that they brought civilization and order to the lands over which they ruled. However, they also respected the gods of the people they conquered.

The most important festival of the Inca year was Inti Raymi, celebrated on December 21, the longest day of the year in the southern

*This silver dish and gold beaker are examples of Inca craftsmanship. Gold was highly prized because it was associated with the sun.*

animals could survive this harsh environment, so the Andean people also ate fish, for which they traded with coastal people, and cuy, a domesticated guinea pig. The llama was a sacred animal to the Incas and often played a role as a sacrificial victim in their religious ceremonies. Beautiful cloth came from llamas' wool, involving the work of herders, shearers, and weavers who produced elaborate patterns.

The well-organized economic system produced a great deal of surplus food, kept in warehouses throughout the empire, which could be distributed in times of shortage. The system required many government bureaucrats and advanced accounting methods. The Incas had no form of writing and used knotted strings to keep records.

In such an immense empire fast transport was essential. All food and

*This 16th-century engraving shows Atahualpa, the Inca emperor, after his capture by the conquistador Francisco Pizarro. Although Atahualpa paid a ransom of gold and silver for his release, the Spanish put him to death and installed a puppet Inca emperor, Manco, in his place.*

hemisphere. Many mummies (*see box*) were brought out to honor the sun. At the end of the festival the Inca emperor and the nobles of Cuzco broke the ground with a digging stick. This signaled the beginning of the new agricultural year.

### THE INCA EMPEROR

The Incas believed that their emperor, himself known as the Inca, was descended from Inti, the sun god. The emperor's costume included several huge solid gold disks in the image of the sun. He and his family also wore large gold earrings that elongated their ears, causing the Spanish to give the Incas the nickname of *orejones*, or "big-eared men."

The Inca rulers were detested by some of the Andean peoples they conquered. They also did not have a secure method for appointing successors. The competition for the imperial throne between the Inca leaders and half-brothers Atahualpa and Huascar sparked civil war in the 1520s. Coupled with a smallpox epidemic, this seriously disrupted

Andean life around the time the Spanish arrived. Although the conquistadors easily eliminated the rulers, they faced many difficulties in destroying all traces of Inca rule.

At first the Spanish set up a puppet Inca ruler in Cuzco called Manco. This led to rebellion, however, and some Inca nobles organized a breakaway kingdom in the jungle that survived into the 1570s. The Spanish also faced many challenges in terms of persistent Inca beliefs. The Incas continued to consider certain mountains and other natural geographic features to be sacred. Since the Spanish could not separate people from such things, the Andean people continued to worship supernatural forces.

The Spanish conquerors were aided by the complex Inca bureaucracy and were even able to live off the surplus food stored in Inca warehouses for years. The Incas were no longer emperors, and Cuzco was no longer an important capital city. However, for many generations descendants of the Incas were regarded as nobility within the Spanish Empire in the Americas.

SEE ALSO

• Colonization
• Conquistadors
• Missionaries
• Latin America
• Spanish Empire

# INDIA

In the 16th and 17th centuries much of India was part of the Muslim Mogul Empire. The empire was founded in 1526 by Babur, sultan of Kabul, when he conquered northwest India. By 1700 the empire covered almost the entire Indian subcontinent.

The founder of the Mogul Empire, Babur (1483–1530), came from Central Asia, the area to the north and northwest of India. He was supposedly descended from two great Mongol conquerors, Genghis Khan (about 1167–1227) and Timur (about 1336–1405), founder of the Timurid Dynasty. At the beginning of the 16th century Babur was one of a number of Timurid princes who fought each other for control of Timur's empire and the surrounding territories in Central Asia. He tried but failed to capture Samarkand in modern Uzbekistan. However, in 1504 he captured Kabul and established a sultanate (a territory under a Muslim ruler) in what is now Afghanistan.

### BABUR'S VICTORIES
In 1519 Babur turned his attention to India and advanced into Punjab in the northwest. At first he was unable to establish control. However, he launched further attacks, and in late 1525 he began to advance eastward through the lands of the Delhi Sultanate, which was ruled by the Afghan Lodi Dynasty. In 1526 Babur defeated the forces of Ibrahim Lodi at Panipat and captured the city of Delhi. The following year he

secured victories over Rajput warriors and took Agra. By the time of his death in 1530 he had reached the border of Bengal (modern Bangladesh) in northeast India and laid the foundations of the Mogul Empire.

Babur was succeeded by his son Humayun (1508–1566), who ruled

*Surrounded by courtiers, Babur talks to a guest within a pavilion set in a garden. Babur built gardens throughout his new territories.*

from 1530 to 1556. Humayan had varied fortunes in India, suffering heavy military defeats in the east at Chausa (1539) and Kannauj (1540) against the Afghan leader Sher Khan. Khan took Delhi, exiled Humayun from India, and built a powerful and well-run empire. However, after his death in 1545 the empire went into decline.

Taking advantage, Humayun pushed back into India in 1554, capturing Lahore in February 1555. By July Delhi and Agra were back in Mogul hands, but in January 1556 Humayan was killed in an accident. His young son Akbar came to the throne. Akbar (1542–1605) would become one of the greatest rulers in the history of India.

### THE REIGN OF AKBAR

In 1556 the Mogul presence in India was under threat from both Afghan armies in the north and internal fighting between Mogul governors. Because of his youth, until 1560 Akbar ruled with the help of a regent (an official who rules on behalf of a monarch), Bayram Khan. By that year a series of major military campaigns had brought the whole of northern India under Akbar's control. Akbar now began to spread his rule through conquest and diplomacy. By 1605, the year of Akbar's death, the Mogul Empire covered two-thirds of the Indian subcontinent, extending as far down as the Deccan in the south and Bengal in the east.

Akbar's success was not just due to military power. He was a wise ruler who made friends while crushing foes. In 1562 he married a princess of the Rajput people of northern India, thus bringing together former enemies. Previous Muslim rulers had often discriminated against or persecuted Hindus. For example, until 1563 Hindus had to pay extra taxes purely

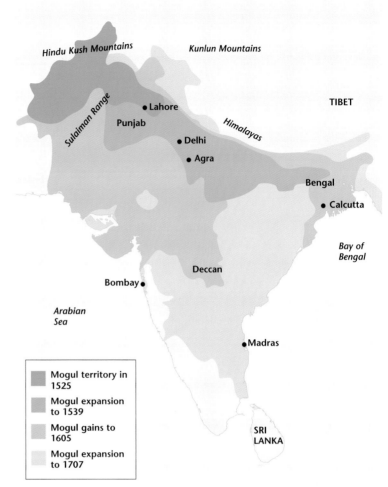

for being Hindu and whenever they went on pilgrimages. Akbar abolished such taxes in the mid 1560s and also allowed Hindus and members of India's non-Mogul peoples to occupy posts in government and rule over local territories. As a result, the only people who rebelled were limited to some backward-looking Mogul tribes or nobles who resented the new situation. A series of revolts by Mogul nobles from 1564 to 1574 was crushed by Akbar, and his power was never seriously threatened again.

Akbar also constructed a modern system of government and finance suited to ruling such a vast territory. The whole empire was divided into 15 provinces, each with its own governor

*This map shows the rise of the Moguls in India from 1525 to 1707.*

and officials. Akbar separated the powers of different departments of government so that no one person had too much influence, so reducing the likelihood of corruption and bad government. He allowed each district to run much of its own affairs, although he remained the absolute ruler. Akbar also introduced a fairer tax system and established a common system of money using copper, silver, and gold coins.

## THE 17TH-CENTURY EMPIRE

After Akbar's death in 1605 the Mogul Empire continued to grow in power and strength. Three great Mogul emperors dominated 17th-century India. Jahangir's reign (1605–1627) was a troubled one, and he was plagued by his children. He immediately had to crush a rebellion headed by his son, Krushaw. In 1606 he fought off an attempt by Shah Abbas I of Persia (present-day Iran) to capture Kandahar in Afghanistan. However, in 1622 the Persians succeeded in taking Kandahar after another of Jahangir's sons, Khurram, began a rebellion. The rebellion failed, and Khurram was hunted by Jahangir's forces. In 1626 he surrendered, and his father forgave him.

Jahangir died in 1627, and Khurram succeeded him. Taking the name Shah Jahan, he ruled from 1628 to 1658, after first killing anyone else who also had a possible claim to the throne. He crushed several rebellions and conquered the troublesome Deccan region in southern India. He also succeeded in taking back Kandahar in 1638.

Among Shah Jahan's greatest achievements were the buildings he commissioned. The most famous of these was the Taj Mahal in Agra. However, he also had two magnificent mosques built in Agra, while in Delhi he was responsible for the building of the Great Mosque and the Red Fort.

In 1657 Shah Jahan fell ill. His sons, Aurangzeb, Shuja, Dara, and Murad then fought a bitter war over the throne from 1657 to 1659. Shah Jahan wanted Dara to succeed him, but it was Aurangzeb who emerged victorious. Aurangzeb imprisoned his father, who eventually died in 1666.

## AURANGZEB'S RULE

Aurangzeb's reign (1658–1707) marked the beginning of the end of the Mogul Empire. The territories of the empire still grew, and by 1707 only the very southern tip of India remained outside

*Shah Jahan, the Mogul ruler of India from 1628 to 1658, sits on his Peacock Throne. The canopy is held up by 12 emerald pillars.*

# ART AND ARCHITECTURE

The stability of the Mogul Empire brought great wealth to many of India's nobles, landowners, and merchants. Much money was spent on luxury goods, and the Mogul period stands out as one of the greatest artistic eras in Indian history. Large concentrations of diamonds in eastern India along with imported silver and gold resulted in exquisite jewelry. Portrait and miniature painting became popular, particularly during the reign of Jahangir. In terms of architecture the most famous Mogul building is the Taj Mahal in Agra, the beautiful mausoleum built under Shah Jahan for his wife Mumtaz. More than 20,000 workmen and craftsmen took 22 years to construct it.

*Standing in a Persian water garden that represents Paradise, the Taj Mahal is one of the most beautiful buildings in the world. It is constructed from white marble and decorated with inlays of semiprecious stones.*

Mogul control. However, despite being intelligent and cultured, Aurangzeb was not a popular ruler. Unlike Akbar, he was not in favor of religious tolerance, and he began to persecute non-Muslims and expel them from government posts. His intolerant rule made him unpopular, and war and rebellion spread throughout the empire. Under these conditions the economy began to decline, people suffered under heavier taxes, and there were plots among the Mogul nobles.

After Aurangzeb died in 1707, the empire went into rapid decline. The Marathas, a peasant warrior people from western Deccan, controlled central India into the late 1700s. But in the 19th century the English defeated them and governed the country.

SEE ALSO
• Akbar
• Central Asia
• Shah Abbas the Great
• Shah Jahan

# INQUISITION

**The Inquisition was an investigative and judicial process set up by the Catholic church in 1231 to seek out suspected heretics (those who held beliefs contrary to church teachings) and interrogate them. Those found guilty of heresy were punished, sometimes by being burned to death.**

The aim of the Inquisition was to correct people's "false" beliefs. The inquisitors were usually friars, who acted both as investigators and judges. At first they concentrated on groups, such as the Albigensians in France, but later they also investigated individuals suspected of witchcraft.

The inquisitors carried out their investigations in a particular area and allowed a period of time for heretics to come and confess their false beliefs. Those who did so received a relatively light punishment, such as paying a fine. Inquisitors encouraged anonymous denunciations of suspected heretics and did not allow the accused to know who had accused him or her. Suspects were rounded up and tried; they might sometimes be tortured to obtain confessions. If found guilty, they could be flogged or burned at the stake.

These methods were justified in theory by the secret, subversive nature of heresy and because heresy was a threat to both religious and civil order. Only unrepentant heretics who refused to confess risked execution—in theory. However, the system encouraged and allowed abuses and excesses.

*An "auto-da-fe" is held on the Plaza Mayor in Madrid on June 30, 1680. This was a highly theatrical public ceremony handing down the sentences of the Inquisition. Convicted heretics were sentenced after walking through the streets wearing yellow shirts emblazoned with red crosses.*

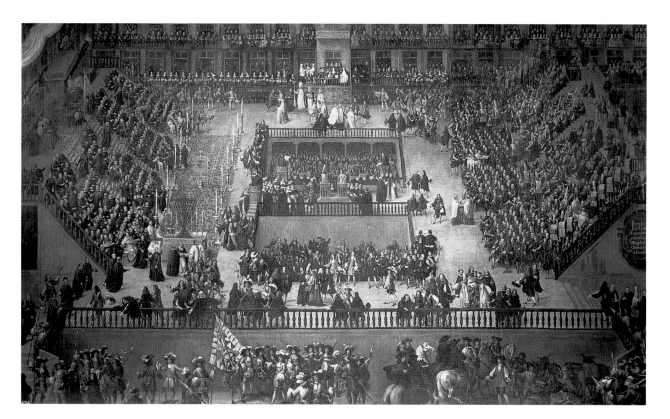

*A torture chamber of the Inquisition is depicted in this painting, dating from about 1710, by the Italian artist Alessandro Magnasco.*

## THE SPANISH INQUISITION

The Spanish Inquisition was founded in 1478. Under Tomás de Torquemada (*see box*) the inquisitors targeted Jewish and Muslim converts to Catholicism who were suspected of secretly reverting to their old faiths. Later the Inquisition sought out Protestants. However, no one was absolutely safe—even devout Catholics, such as Teresa of Avila, were investigated for heresy. The Inquisition also operated in the Spanish colonies in the Americas. It was finally abolished in Spain in 1834.

## THE ROMAN INQUISITION

An Inquisition was set up in Rome in 1542. Also known as the Holy Office, the Roman Inquisition initially aimed to stop the spread of Protestantism. However, it soon turned its attention to Catholics suspected of heresy, especially academics. Among its victims were the scientist Galileo Galilei, who was sentenced to house arrest, and the philosopher Giordano Bruno, who was burned at the stake. While the Roman Inquisition achieved its aim of stamping out Protestantism—there were practically no Protestants left in Italy by 1600—it also seriously limited the expression of new ideas.

## GRAND INQUISITOR

Perhaps the most notorious figure of the Spanish Inquisition, Tomás de Torquemada (1420–1498) was responsible for the deaths of thousands of victims. Some historians emphasize that he was a product of his times—that his use of torture was not unusual, and that he was not so much sadistic and cruel as rigorous at his job. However, some 2,000 people were burned during his years as grand inquisitor.

Torquemada was a Dominican from the city of Valladolid in north-central Spain. He became confessor to the monarchs Ferdinand and Isabella, and so was able to wield considerable influence at court. In 1483 he was appointed grand inquisitor to organize the Inquisition. He set up five tribunals around the country as well as a supreme council. In 1484 Torquemada drew up guidelines for inquisitors that remained in force for the next three centuries. During his time in office thousands of people were imprisoned, had their property confiscated, or were put to death. He was also the driving force behind the decision in 1492 to expel from Spain all Jews who refused to become Christians.

SEE ALSO

- Catholic church
- Galileo Galilei
- Heresy and heretics
- Jews and Judaism
- Religious dissent
- Teresa of Avila
- Violence

# INVENTIONS AND INVENTORS

**Between 1500 and 1700 a number of important inventions, including the microscope and telescope, helped push back the boundaries of science. Toward the end of the period scientific experiments with gases and vacuums led to the development of the steam engine.**

During the 1500s scientists began to observe the natural world more closely instead of relying on traditional theories. Two inventions essential to this study were the telescope and microscope. These instruments enabled people to see the natural world in much greater detail than with the naked eye. Both were based on lenses—curved pieces of glass that alter the path of rays of light as they pass through them. Lenses can be used to magnify tiny or distant objects.

### THE MICROSCOPE
The first microscopes had a lens at one end and a plate, on which to place the object to be examined, at the other. They had a magnification of less than 10 times the actual size of the object. These early microscopes were used to look at small insects such as fleas and so were dubbed "flea glasses." The Dutch eyeglass maker Hans Janssen and his son Zacharias (1580–about 1638) are credited with making the first compound microscope in the 1590s. This instrument used two lenses and gave a magnification of up to 20 times the size of the object.

Two men popularized microscopes and used them to observe and describe microscopic organisms. One was the

Dutchman Anton van Leeuwenhoek (1632–1723). He used a simple microscope with a single lens but developed a way of grinding and polishing very high-quality lenses that magnified objects by up to 300 times. He was the first person to see and describe bacteria, the microorganisms in a drop of water, and the circulation of blood cells. The English scientist Robert Hooke (1635–1703) lived at the same time as van Leeuwenhoek and was, like him, a member of the Royal Society in London. He

*A 17th-century microscope thought to have belonged to the scientist Robert Hooke. Also shown are a lens box and an instrument to light the specimen.*

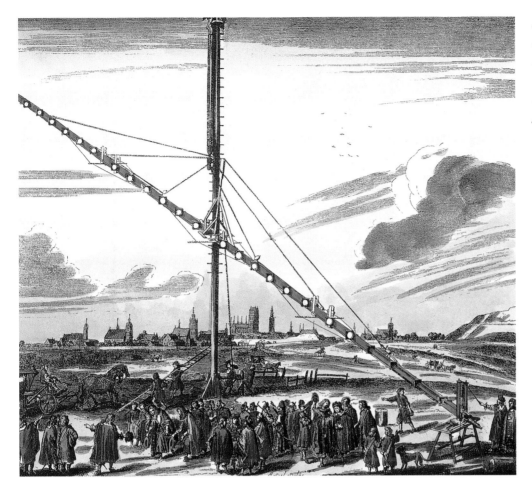

*A crowd watches as a giant telescope belonging to the 17th-century Polish astronomer Johannes Hevelius is hoisted into place in this print made in 1673. Hevelius designed his own instruments to study the skies, including this telescope that measured some 150 ft (45m) long.*

improved the design of compound microscopes and published his observations in 1665 under the title *Micrographia* (Small Drawings)—a book that was probably the original inspiration for van Leeuwenhoek. Hooke later confirmed the Dutchman's discoveries. He also coined the term "cell" for the microscopic cavities that he observed in a slice of cork.

## THE TELESCOPE

The telescope was probably invented in the 1590s in the Netherlands, although the identity of its inventor is unknown. In 1608 the Dutch eyeglass maker Hans Lippershey (about 1570–about 1619) demonstrated a telescope. He thought that it would be useful for military purposes. The Italian scientist Galileo Galilei (1564–1642) heard of the new invention and in 1609 built his own improved telescope with a focusing device. He used it to observe the skies and became the first person to see the craters on the moon, sunspots, and the four moons of Jupiter. There were several problems with these early refracting, or Galilean, telescopes. Galileo's telescope had a limited magnification of up to 30 times. It also gave a very narrow view—he could see only one quarter of the moon at one time. The glass lenses used in the early refracting telescopes also produced distorted images.

The English scientist Isaac Newton (1642–1727) built an improved design in 1668, based on ideas of the Scottish inventor James Gregory (1638–1675). This type of telescope, known as a reflecting telescope, used a curved mirror to collect light and reflect it back to a point of focus, instead of using several lenses. Newton's design meant that larger telescopes could be built that magnified objects many millions of times.

## MEASURING HEAT

Galileo was one of a circle of learned men in Venice who made a remarkable number of inventions, including early thermometers known as thermoscopes. Several men are credited with inventing these instruments, but Galileo's friend Santorio Santorio (1561–1636) was the first to add a numerical scale. The German scientist Daniel Fahrenheit (1686–1736) invented the alcohol thermometer in 1709. Five years later he invented the mercury thermometer and in 1724 the Fahrenheit scale, both of which are still used today.

*A man holds up an early watch in this portrait painted in about 1558. A detached alarm mechanism and its case lie on the table. The first watches were made around 1500 when the locksmith Peter Henlein introduced the mainspring as a replacement for weights in driving clocks. Early clocks and watches had only an hour hand.*

## CLOCKS AND WATCHES

In around 1500 the German locksmith Peter Henlein made the first portable clock in Nuremberg, Germany. The accuracy of clocks was much improved by the Dutch inventor Christiaan Huygens (1629–1695). In 1656 he designed the first pendulum clock, which was accurate to within one minute a day. He later reduced the margin of error to 10 seconds a day.

In the mid-1670s Huygens invented the balance wheel and spring assembly, a mechanism that made portable clocks and watches accurate to within 10 minutes a day. He gave the first watch regulated by this mechanism to the French King Louis XIV, who had invited him to Paris to help found the French Academy of Sciences in 1666.

Huygens made many contributions to the world of science. His inventions included huge telescopes with focal lengths of up to 210 ft (64m) and an eyepiece for a telescope. He also planned—but never built—an internal combustion engine powered by gunpowder in 1680.

## THE STEAM ENGINE

The French inventor Denis Papin (1647–about 1712) helped Huygens with his experiments with gunpowder engines. He decided to apply the same principles to steam. In 1679 Papin invented a pressure cooker that was the precursor of one of the most important inventions of all time: the steam engine. Steam engines convert heat into motion, which can then be used to drive pumps or other machines. They operate by using the heat energy to boil water into steam. This causes a change in volume that drives a piston to produce motion.

Several scientific discoveries in the 16th and 17th centuries led to the invention of the steam engine. They

# IMPORTANT INVENTIONS FROM 1500 TO 1700

1504 German locksmith Peter Henlein makes the first portable timepieces.

1550 Gunsmiths and armorers invent the screwdriver. The first wrench was also made this year.

1595 Dutch eyeglass makers Hans Janssen and his son Zacharias invent the compound microscope.

1608 Dutch eyeglass maker Hans Lippershey demonstrates the telescope.

1609 Italian scientist Galileo Galilei builds a telescope and uses it for for astronomy.

1614 Scottish mathematician John Napier formulates the theory of logarithms, which helps multiply and divide large numbers.

1622 English mathematician William Oughtred constructs the first slide rule, a device for calculating numbers.

1642 Frenchman Blaise Pascal invents the first mechanical calculator for adding and subtraction.

1643 Italian scientists Evangelista Torricelli and Vincenzo Viviani invent the barometer for measuring air pressure.

1656 Dutch scientist Christiaan Huygens invents the pendulum clock.

1660 German scientist Otto von Guericke uses the barometer to predict weather.

1671 German intellectual Gottfried Wilhelm Leibniz modifies Pascal's calculator to divide and multiply.

include the English scientist Robert Boyle's (1627–1691) investigations of gases and the German scientist Otto von Guericke's (1602–1686) work on pressure and vacuums.

In 1698 the English military engineer Thomas Savery (about 1650–1715) took out a patent for an invention based on Papin's pressure cooker. His engine gave "motion to all sorts of mill work by the impellent force of fire." The English engineer Thomas Newcomen (1663–1729) built the first practical machine in 1712 to pump water from mine shafts. The widespread use of the steam engine in the following century led to the Industrial Revolution in England.

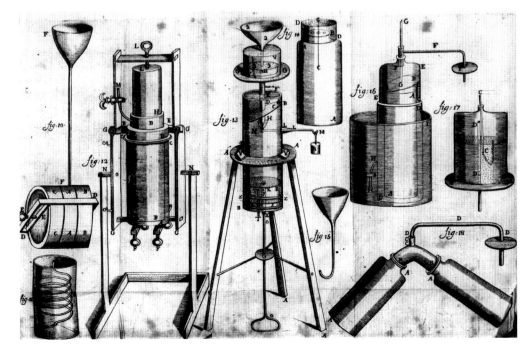

*These illustrations made in 1681 show the "steam digester," or pressure cooker, designed by the French scientist Denis Papin.*

SEE ALSO

- Astronomy
- Clocks and calendars
- Galileo Galilei
- Mathematics
- Science
- Technology

# TIMELINE

♦ **1492** Christopher Columbus lands in the Bahamas, claiming the territory for Spain.

♦ **1494** Charles VIII of France invades Italy, beginning four decades of Italian wars.

♦ **1494** The Treaty of Tordesillas divides the "new world" between Spain and Portugal.

♦ **1498** Portuguese navigator Vasco da Gama sails around Africa to reach Calicut, India.

♦ **1509** Dutch humanist scholar Desiderius Erasmus publishes *In Praise of Folly*, a satire on religion and society.

♦ **1511** The Portuguese capture Melaka in Southeast Asia.

♦ **1515** Francis I of France invades Italy, capturing Milan.

♦ **1516** Charles, grandson of Holy Roman emperor Maximilian I, inherits the Spanish throne as Charles I.

♦ **1517** The German monk Martin Luther nails his Ninety-five Theses to a church door in Wittenberg, Germany, setting the Reformation in motion.

♦ **1518** The Portuguese begin trading in slaves from Africa.

♦ **1519** Charles I of Spain is elected Holy Roman emperor as Charles V.

♦ **1519–1521** Spanish conquistador Hernán Cortés conquers Mexico for Spain.

♦ **1520** Suleyman the Magnificent becomes sultan of the Ottoman Empire.

♦ **1520** Portuguese navigator Ferdinand Magellan rounds the tip of South America and is the first European to sight the Pacific Ocean.

♦ **1521** Pope Leo X excommunicates Martin Luther.

♦ **1521** At the Diet of Worms, Luther refuses to recant his views. The Holy Roman emperor outlaws him.

♦ **1522** One of Magellan's ships completes the first circumnavigation of the globe.

♦ **1523** Gustav Vasa becomes king of Sweden and dissolves the Kalmar Union that had dominated Scandinavia.

♦ **1523–1525** Huldrych Zwingli sets up a reformed church in Zurich, Switzerland.

♦ **1525** Holy Roman Emperor Charles V defeats and captures Francis I of France at the Battle of Pavia.

♦ **1525** In Germany the Peasants' Revolt is crushed; its leaders, including the radical Thomas Münzer, are executed.

♦ **1525** William Tyndale translates the New Testament into English.

♦ **1526** Mongol leader Babur invades northern India and establishes the Mogul Empire.

♦ **1526** At the Diet of Speyer German princes are granted the authority to allow Lutheran teachings and worship in their own territories.

♦ **1526** Suleyman the Magnificent defeats Hungarian forces at the Battle of Mohács.

♦ **1527** Charles V's forces overrun Italy and sack Rome.

♦ **1529** In the Peace of Cambrai with Charles V, Francis I of France renounces all French claims in Italy temporarily confirming Spanish supremacy.

♦ **1529** The Ottoman sultan Suleyman the Magnificent besieges the city of Vienna.

♦ **1531** German Protestant princes form the Schmalkaldic League to defend themselves.

♦ **1531–1532** Spanish conquistador Francisco Pizarro conquers Peru for Spain by defeating the Inca Empire.

♦ **1532** Niccolò Machiavelli's *The Prince* is published.

♦ **1534** The earl of Kildare, Thomas Lord Offaly, leads a revolt against Henry VIII's rule in Ireland.

♦ **1534** Henry VIII of England breaks away from the authority of the pope and establishes the Church of England.

♦ **1534** Martin Luther publishes his German translation of the New Testament.

♦ **1535–1536** The city of Geneva adopts Protestantism and expels all Catholic clergy.

♦ **1536** Henry VIII orders the dissolution of the monasteries.

♦ **1536** John Calvin publishes his *Institutes of the Christian Religion*, which sets out central Protestant principles.

♦ **1539** Ignatius Loyola founds the Society of Jesus (Jesuits).

♦ **1541** John Calvin sets up a model Christian community in Geneva, Switzerland.

♦ **1542** Pope Paul III reestablishes the Inquisition, a medieval religious court designed to combat heresy.

♦ **1543** The Flemish anatomist Andreas Vesalius publishes his handbook of anatomy *On the Structure of the Human Body*.

♦ **1543** Polish astronomer Nicolaus Copernicus publishes *On the Revolutions of the Heavenly Orbs*, which challenged contemporary beliefs by describing a sun-centered universe.

♦ **1545** Pope Paul III organizes the Council of Trent to counter the threat of Protestantism and reinvigorate the church.

♦ **1547** Ivan IV (the Terrible) becomes czar of Russia.

♦ **1547** Charles V defeats the Schmalkaldic League at the Battle of Mühlberg.

♦ **1553** Mary I restores the Catholic church in England.

♦ **1555** In the Peace of Augsburg Charles V allows German princes to decide the religion in their territories.

♦ **1555** Charles V abdicates, dividing his vast lands between his brother Ferdinand and son Philip.

♦ **1558** On the death of Mary I, her half-sister Elizabeth I becomes queen of England.

♦ **1559** Elizabeth I restores the Church of England.

♦ **1559** Pope Paul IV institutes the Index of Prohibited Books.

♦ **1562** The Wars of Religion break out in France.

♦ **1563** The Council of Trent ends having clarified Catholic doctrine and laid the basis of the Counter Reformation.

♦ **1566** The Dutch begin a revolt against Spanish rule.

♦ **1569** Flemish cartographer Gerardus Mercator publishes a world map using a new method of projection.

♦ **1571** Philip II of Spain leads an allied European force to victory over the Ottomans at the naval Battle of Lepanto.

♦ **1572** French Catholics murder thousands of Protestants across France in the Saint Bartholomew's Day Massacre.

♦ **1579** Seven Dutch provinces form the Union of Utrecht to fight for independence from Spanish rule.

♦ **1582** The warlord Toyotomi Hideyoshi becomes effective ruler of Japan.

♦ **1588** Philip II launches the Armada invasion fleet against England, but it is destroyed.

♦ **1590** Toyotomi Hideyoshi expels Christian missionaries from Japan.

♦ **1593** The English playwright William Shakespeare publishes his first work, *Venus and Adonis* beginning his prolific and successful career in the theater.

♦ **1598** The Persian Safavid ruler Shah Abbas the Great moves his capital to Esfahan.

♦ **1598** In the Edict of Nantes Henry IV of France grants Huguenots considerable rights, bringing an end to the French Wars of Religion.

♦ **1600** The English East India Company is founded in London to control trade with India and East Asia.

♦ **1602** The Dutch government establishes the Dutch East India Company.

♦ **1603** In Japan Tokugawa Ieyasu unites the country under his rule as shogun, ushering in a age of peace and prosperity.

♦ **1603** James VI of Scotland also becomes king of England as James I on the death of Elizabeth I.

♦ **1605** The Gunpowder Plot: A group of Catholics including Guy Fawkes fail to blow up the English Parliament.

♦ **1607** Henry Hudson sails to the Barents Sea in search of a northeastern passage to Asia.

♦ **1607** John Smith founds the English colony of Jamestown in Virginia.

♦ **1611** James I's authorized Bible, the King James Version, is published.

♦ **1616** Cardinal Richelieu becomes the prime minister of France.

♦ **1618** The Defenestration of Prague marks the beginning of the Thirty Years' War.

♦ **1620** The *Mayflower* pilgrims found the colony of New Plymouth in Massachusetts.

♦ **1621** Huguenots (French Protestants) rebel against King Louis XIII of France.

♦ **1625** Charles I is crowned king of England.

♦ **1629** Charles I dissolves Parliament and rules independently until 1640.

♦ **1631** The Mogul Emperor Shah Jahan builds the Taj Mahal as a mausoleum for his wife Mumtaz.

♦ **1632** Galileo Galilei publishes his *Dialogue Concerning the Two Chief World Systems*, in which he supports Copernicus's views of a sun-centered universe.

♦ **1633** Galileo is tried for heresy and sentenced to house arrest by the Roman Inquisition.

♦ **1637–1638** After a rebellion led by Christians in Japan 37,000 Japanese Christians are executed and many Europeans expelled from the country.

♦ **1640** Portuguese peasants rebel against Spanish rule and declare John of Braganza their king. Portugal finally regains its independence in 1668.

♦ **1641** French philosopher René Descartes publishes one of his most important works, *Meditations on First Philosophy*.

♦ **1642** Civil war breaks out in England between the king and Parliament.

♦ **1642** Jules Mazarin follows Cardinal Richelieu to become prime minister of France.

♦ **1643** Louis XIV becomes king of France. During his reign France becomes powerful.

♦ **1648** The Thirty Years' War comes to an end with the Treaty of Westphalia.

♦ **1648–1653** The Fronde, a series of civil wars, breaks out in France.

♦ **1649** The English king Charles I is executed and England becomes a republic.

♦ **1652** England and the Dutch Republic clash in the first Anglo-Dutch Naval War.

♦ **1653** The English Puritan Oliver Cromwell dissolves Parliament and rules England as lord protector.

♦ **1660** The English Parliament restores Charles II as king.

♦ **1660** The Royal Society of London is founded to promote scientific enquiry.

♦ **1661** Louis XIV begins work on the palace of Versailles outside Paris.

♦ **1661** Manchu Emperor Kang-hsi comes to power in China. His long reign marks a golden age in Chinese history.

♦ **1665** The Great Plague in London kills around a thousand people every week.

♦ **1666** French minister Jean-Baptiste Colbert establishes the French Academy to promote the sciences.

♦ **1666** The Great Fire of London destroys a large part of the English capital.

♦ **1670** The English Hudson's Bay Company is founded to occupy lands and trade in North America.

♦ **1678** English Puritan writer John Bunyan publishes his hugely popular allegorical book *Pilgrim's Progress*.

♦ **1683** The Turkish Ottoman army besieges Vienna for the second time.

♦ **1685** Louis XIV revokes the Edict of Nantes, depriving French Protestants of all religious and civil liberties. Hundreds of thousands of Huguenots flee France.

♦ **1688** In the Glorious Revolution the Protestant Dutch leader, William of Orange, is invited to replace James II as king of England.

♦ **1689** The Bill of Rights establishes a constitutional monarchy in England. William III and his wife Mary II jointly rule England and Scotland.

♦ **1694** The Bank of England is founded in London.

♦ **1699** Turks withdraw from Austria and Hungary.

♦ **1700–1721** The Great Northern War between Sweden and Russia and its allies weakens Swedish power.

♦ **1701** The War of the Spanish Succession breaks out over the vacant Spanish throne.

♦ **1704** Isaac Newton publishes his book *Optics* on the theory of light and color.

♦ **1707** The Act of Union unites England and Scotland. The seat of Scottish government is moved to London.

♦ **1712** Peter the Great makes Saint Petersburg the new capital of Russia, beginning a period of westernization.

♦ **1713–1714** The treaties of Utrecht are signed by England and France, ending the War of the Spanish Succession.

♦ **1715** The sun king King Louis XIV of France dies, marking the end of a golden age in French culture.

# GLOSSARY

**Absolutism**
A system of government in which far-reaching power is held by a monarch or ruler over his or her subjects.

**Alchemy**
A tradition of investigative thought that tried to explain the relationship between humanity and the universe and exploit it, for example, by finding a way to turn base metal into gold.

**Baroque**
An artistic style originating in the 17th century characterized by dramatic effects and ornamentation, which aimed to evoke a strong emotional response.

**Calvinists**
Followers of the French Protestant reformer John Calvin. Calvinism emphasized the sovereignty of God and predestination—the idea that that God decided in advance who would gain eternal life.

**Counter Reformation**
The Catholic church's efforts to reinvigorate itself, bring an end to abuses, clarify its teachings, and prevent the spread of Protestantism.

**Diet**
An assembly of the rulers of the Holy Roman Empire, who gathered to pass laws and make important decisions.

**Doctrine**
A specific principle or belief, or system of beliefs, taught by a religious faith.

**Elector**
A leading landowner in the Holy Roman Empire who had a vote in the election of the Holy Roman emperor.

**Enclosure**
A process by which major landowners extended their holdings across common land.

**Excommunication**
A punishment in which a person was banned from taking part in the rites of the Catholic church.

**Franciscans**
Members of a Catholic religious order founded in the early 13th century by Saint Francis of Assisi.

**Guild**
An association of merchants, professionals, or craftsmen organized to protect the interests of its members and to regulate the quality and cost of their services.

**Heresy**
A belief that is contrary to the teachings of a religious faith.

**Huguenots**
The name given to Calvinists in France.

**Humanism**
An academic approach based on the study of "humanities"—that is, ancient Greek and Roman texts, history, and philosophy—which stressed the importance of developing rounded, cultured individuals.

**Iconoclasm**
The destruction of religious objects, usually by those who disapproved of the use of images in worship.

**Indulgences**
The cancelation or reduction of punishments for sins granted by the Catholic church in return for good works or money.

**Inquisition**
A powerful medieval religious court that was revived by the Catholic church in the 16th century to stamp out ideas contrary to Catholic teachings.

**Janissaries**
Members of an elite infantry corps in the Ottoman army.

**Jesuits**
Members of a Catholic order founded in the 16th century by Ignatius Loyola. They were famous for their work as educators and missionaries.

**Laity or laypeople**
Members of a religious faith who are not clergy.

**Lutherans**
Followers of the German Protestant reformer Martin Luther. He protested against abuses in the Catholic church and argued that the scriptures, not church traditions, were the ultimate religious authority.

**Mass or Eucharist**
A key Christian sacrament of thanksgiving for the sacrifice of Jesus's life celebrated with wine and bread representing his body and blood.

**Mercantilism**
An economic system under which a government regulated manufacturing and trade in the belief that high exports and low imports would enrich the country's treasury and make the state powerful.

**Mercenary**
A soldier who fights for any employer in return for wages.

**Papacy**
The pope and his advisers in Rome who govern the Catholic church.

**Patriarch**
The title given to Orthodox church leaders: The most important patriarchs were the bishops of Antioch, Rome, Alexandria, Constantinople, and Jerusalem.

**Patron**
Someone who orders and pays for a work of art or supports, usually financially, the work of an artist or thinker.

**Protestant**
Someone who follows one of the Christian churches set up during the Reformation in reaction to the corruption of the Catholic church.

**Sacrament**
An important Christian ritual, or ceremony, such as Mass or baptism. The number and nature of the sacraments were issues of major debate during the Reformation.

**Secular**
A term to describe something nonreligious as opposed to something religious.

**Theology**
The study of religion.

**Tithe**
A tax of one-tenth of a person's annual produce or income payable to the church.

**Usury**
The practice of making a dishonest profit, such as charging high interest on a loan, which was considered sinful by the medieval church.

**Vernacular**
The everyday language spoken by the people of a country or region, rather than a literary or formal language such as Latin.

# FURTHER READING

Barry, J., M. Hester, and G. Roberts (eds.). *Witchcraft in Early Modern Europe: Studies in Culture and Belief.* New York: Cambridge University Press, 1996.

Black, C. F. *Church, Religion, and Society in Early Modern Italy.* New York: Palgrave, 2001.

Boorstin, Daniel J. *The Discoverers.* New York: Harry N. Abrams, 1991.

Collinson, Patrick. *The Reformation: A History.* New York: Modern Library, 2004.

Darby, G. (ed.). *The Origins and Development of the Dutch Revolt.* New York: Routledge, 2001.

Dixon, C. S. *The Reformation in Germany.* Malden, Mass.: Blackwell Publishers, 2002.

Duffy, Eamon. *Saints and Sinners: A History of the Popes.* New Haven, Conn.: Yale University Press, 1997.

Elliott , J. H. *Europe Divided 1559–1598.* Second edition, Malden, Mass.: Blackwell Publishers, 2000.

Gäbler, U., and R.C.L. Gritsch (trans.). *Huldrych Zwingli: His Life and Work.* Philadelphia: Fortress Press, 1998.

Goodwin, Jason. *Lords of the Horizons: A History of the Ottoman Empire.* New York: Henry Holt, 1999.

Henry, J. *The Scientific Revolution and the Origins of Modern Science.* Second edition, New York: Palgrave, 2001.

Jaffer, Amin, and Anna Jackson (eds.). *Encounters: The Meeting of Asia and Europe 1500–1800.* New York: Harry N. Abrams, 2004.

Jewell, Helen M. *Education in Early Modern England.* New York: St. Martin's Press, 1998.

Jones, M. D. W. *The Counter Reformation: Religion and Society in Early Modern Europe.* New York: Cambridge University Press, 1995.

Klein, Herbert S. *The Atlantic Slave Trade.* New York: Cambridge University Press, 1999.

Kuhn, Thomas S. *The Copernican Revolution.* New York: MJF Books, 1997.

Lane, Kris. *Pillaging the Empire: Piracy in the Americas, 1500–1750.* Armok, NY: M. E. Sharpe, 1998.

Lindberg, Carter (ed.). *The European Reformation Sourcebook.* Malden, Mass.: Blackwell Publishers, 1999.

MacCulloch, Diarmaid. *The Reformation: A History.* New York: Viking Press, 2004.

Marius, R. *Martin Luther: The Christian between God and Death.* Cambridge, Mass.: Belknap Press, 1999.

McGrath, A. E. *Reformation Thought.* Third edition, Malden, Mass.: Blackwell Publishers, 1999.

Oakley, S. P. *War and Peace in the Baltic 1560–1790.* New York: Routledge, 1992.

Porter, Roy. *The Greatest Benefit to Mankind: Medical History of Humanity.* New York: W. W. Norton, 1998.

Rawlings, Helen. *The Spanish Inquisition.* Malden, Mass.: Blackwell Publishers, 2005.

*Renaissance.* Danbury, Connecticut: Grolier, 2002.

Roth, Mitchel P. *Crime and Punishment: A History of the Criminal Justice System.* Belmont, CA: Thomson Wadsworth, 2005.

Russell-Wood, A. J. R. *The Portuguese Empire, 1415–1808: A World on the Move.* Baltimore, MD: Johns Hopkins University Press, 1998.

Schama, Simon. *The Embarrassment of Riches: Dutch Culture in the Golden Age.* New York: Vintage Books, 1997.

Stoyle, John. *Europe Unfolding 1648–1688.* Second edition, Malden, Mass.: Blackwell Publishers, 2000.

Taylor, Alan. *American Colonies: The Settlement of North America to 1800.* New York: Penguin Books, 2003.

Tracy, J. D. *Europe's Reformations 1450–1650.* Lanham: Rowman & Littlefield, 1999.

Walvin, James. *The Quakers: Money and Morals.* London: John Murray, 1997.

Ware, Timothy. *The Orthodox Church.* New York: Penguin Books, 2004.

Wilson, P. H. *The Holy Roman Empire, 1495–1806.* New York: St. Martin's Press, 1999.

**WEBSITES**

*BBC Online: History*
www.bbc.co.uk/history

*British Civil Wars, Commonwealth, and Protectorate 1638–1660*
www.british-civil-wars.co.uk

*Catholic Encyclopedia*
www.newadvent.org/cathen/

*Database of Reformation Artists*
www.artcyclopedia.com/index.html

*History of Protestantism*
www.doctrine.org/history/

*The Library of Economics and Liberty*
www.econlib.org

*National Gallery of Art*
www.nga.gov

*National Maritime Museum, Greenwich*
www.nmm.ac.uk

*Reformation History*
www.historychannel.com

# SET INDEX

# PICTURE CREDITS